Praise for *The Drama Years*

"*The Drama Years* is a great overall primer for anyone with a young teen girl in her life. And the girls will love reading it too! I will highly recommend it to the parents, teachers, and girls I work with."
— Rosalind Wiseman, author of *Queen Bees and Wannabes*

"*The Drama Years* is a wonderful, compassionate, and extremely helpful book. It is a must for any parent with a middle-school-age daughter. Haley Kilpatrick tells it exactly—word for word—as it is. She understands what they are going through, and she gives truly helpful and specific advice. The book is upbeat while at the same time it deals with all of the toughest issues that young teenage girls must face. All parents of young teen girls will love it."
— Anthony E. Wolf, Ph.D., author of *Get Out of My Life,*
But First Could You Drive Me & Cheryl to the Mall?

"Even the closest of parent-child relationships can benefit from this book. The more we listen, the more we help to raise a generation of self-empowered, confident women."
— Lucy Danziger, *SELF* magazine editor-in-chief and author
of *The Drop 10 Diet* and *The Nine Rooms of Happiness*

"*The Drama Years* is filled with heart-stirring stories, just-been-there advice from recent teens, and practical, actionable tips for parents. It's full of real girls talking about everything from stress and body image to love and materialism. Reading this book, I cringed in recognition of my own drama years, just wishing this book had been around back then and so grateful I'll have it as a guide for my own daughter."

—Melissa Walker, cofounder of I Heart Daily
and author of *Small Town Sinners*

"A must-read for any parent struggling to understand her tween daughter and all the 'drama' in her life. Haley Kilpatrick tells it from a girl's perspective with real solutions for grownups."

—Chandra Turner, executive editor, *Parents* magazine

"Pre-teen years are so tough for girls, and adults often aren't sure how best to help. Thankfully, we have the middle school and high school girls who share their hearts and minds in these pages to guide us, telling parents exactly what will help them survive 'The Drama Years.'"

—Julie Foudy, former captain of the U.S. Women's Soccer Team
and founder of Julie Foudy Sports Leadership Academy

*f*P

THE DRAMA YEARS

Real Girls Talk About Surviving Middle School—
Bullies, Brands, Body Image, and More

HALEY KILPATRICK

with Whitney Joiner

FREE PRESS

New York   London   Toronto   Sydney   New Delhi

FREE PRESS
A Division of Simon & Schuster, Inc.
1230 Avenue of the Americas
New York, NY 10020

First Free Press trade paperback edition April 2012

FREE PRESS and colophon are trademarks of Simon & Schuster, Inc.

For information about special discounts for bulk purchases,
please contact Simon & Schuster Special Sales at 1-866-506-1949
or business@simonandschuster.com.

The Simon & Schuster Speakers Bureau can bring authors to your live event.
For more information or to book an event contact the Simon & Schuster Speakers
Bureau at 1-866-248-3049 or visit our website at www.simonspeakers.com.

Manufactured in the United States of America

1   3   5   7   9   10   8   6   4   2

Library of Congress Cataloging-in-Publication Data
Kilpatrick, Haley.
The drama years: real girls talk about surviving middle school—
bullies, brands, body image, and more / Haley Kilpatrick, Whitney Joiner.
p. cm.
Includes bibliographical references and index.
1. Teenage girls. 2. Bullying in schools. 3. Middle schools.
I. Joiner, Whitney. II. Title.
HQ798 .K514 2012
305.235—dc23   2011045076

ISBN 978-1-4516-2791-6
ISBN 978-1-4516-2792-3 (ebook)

To everyone who believes
that today's middle school girls
will become tomorrow's inspiring women

Contents

Contents

Introduction

"Middle school is the hardest thing you'll ever have to go through, probably. In sixth grade, they back-stab you. Seventh grade is all drama, drama, drama. Eighth grade, you don't know who you want to be yet, but you have to know, because high school is the place where you have to have your group."

—Emma, twelve, New Jersey

"In elementary school, it felt like everyone was my friend. But once you get into middle school, your body starts changing; you start getting pimples. There's gossip about who's dating who and social cliques. I was like, `Well, okay . . . I guess this is the way it is now.'"

—Rebecca, thirteen, Texas

It's not easy to be a middle school girl today. In the few years between grade school and high school, girls go through an incredible number of changes, making this the most formative—and riskiest—time in their lives. And though it might not be the hardest thing your tween will ever go through, as Emma, the twelve-year-old quoted above,

1

claims, surviving middle school can feel like the biggest challenge your girl has faced thus far.

School has now become a social minefield for her. A girl's list of friends fluctuates on a regular basis: groups form and turn on each other; classmates gossip about who's saying what to whom; childhood friends tell trusted secrets to others; and just deciding where to sit in the lunchroom can be a daily struggle. She's also experiencing a wave of biological changes—growth spurts, new curves, new hormones—and suddenly she has more grown-up things to worry about too, like dealing with crushes and negotiating how she feels about her body and her appearance. Not to mention that she's also going through a personality crisis, trying to define who she is as an individual, while also desperately trying to fit in with her friends and classmates. And throughout it all, the media are bombarding girls with contradictory and utterly confusing messages, like "act sexy, but don't *do* anything sexual."

To both parents and their girls, the transition from elementary school to middle school often feels like much more than a three-month summer recess; it might as well be a period of many years. Suddenly *everything* is changing, and as part of the natural development process, parents aren't as involved in the classroom as they were during elementary school. Out of nowhere, these girls are expected to grow up and decide who they want to be—and fast.

"Middle school is much tougher than grade school, because the whole identity piece is huge. 'Who do I want to be?' They're really trying to figure it out. They don't want to be the little kid anymore, but they really have no ability to navigate the world in the way they think they can."

—Kris, middle school counselor

Introduction

Recently the world of middle school girls has become even more challenging. More than ever before, these girls feel they must be "perfect"—in school, in sports and other after-school activities, and at home. With more and more girls reporting that they feel severely stressed, this increasing pressure is having a negative effect on their emotional and physical health.

The drive for perfection has dovetailed with our culture's heightened emphasis on appearance—resulting in ever younger girls feeling pressured to conform to an unreasonable standard of beauty and thinness, striving to be pretty, to be "hot" (even as a preteen), to stay in their friends' good graces, and to get the attention of boys.

But without question, the biggest shift in the world of middle school girls is technological. With smart phones, Skype, Gchat, texting, and Facebook, girls in sixth through eighth grade today have more opportunities to connect with others than any previous generation. It's now effortless to anonymously bully someone over the Internet and harass another person through a text message. And it's not just harmful among the girls themselves; studies have shown that our reliance on, and obsession with, technology has decreased the amount of time girls spend with their families. It's becoming more apparent that girls who've grown up with a cell phone available around the clock have a harder time making decisions on their own and trusting their instincts than girls in the past. After all, why not just text Mom or your friends to ask their advice rather than figuring it out on your own?

I've dedicated my life to helping these girls deal with tough issues, so I see firsthand, every day, how scary today's middle school world can be. Guiding you—parents and other mentors of middle school girls—through these tricky waters is what *The Drama Years* is all about.

I'm Haley Kilpatrick, the founder and executive director of a national nonprofit organization called Girl Talk. It's a peer-to-peer mentoring program in which high school girls mentor middle school girls, advising and inspiring them from a "just been there" perspective. I started Girl Talk in 2002, when I was fifteen years old, and in ten years we've grown from the first chapter (in my Georgia school, with forty-five girls) to chapters in forty-three states and six countries, involving more than 40,000 girls. And we're still growing.

I started Girl Talk because middle school was such a hard time for me. (You'll hear a lot more about this throughout the book.) And once my little sister started sixth grade, I could see she was about to go through three tough years too. I knew I couldn't save her from the pain I'd experienced, but I had to try to make it easier somehow—for her, her friends, and other middle school girls.

Here's my background: I grew up in Albany, Georgia, a small city south of Atlanta. I felt like my life was pretty normal; I lived with my mom, dad, younger brother, and younger sister, I did well in school, loved to dance, got along with everyone in my class, and hung out with my best friend, Maryashley. But that all changed during sixth grade when Maryashley's family moved away over spring break.

I tried to get closer to some of the girls I'd known since elementary school—girls who had, by now, formed our grade's popular crowd—but they seemed to despise me. And I had no idea why. I'd head toward an open spot in the lunchroom, only to watch some girl throw her purse down on the empty chair, letting me know that I wasn't welcome. On Mondays, I'd overhear the details of birthday parties that I hadn't been invited to over the weekend. Yet sometimes they would unexpectedly be nice to me, and I would think we were friends. The constant back and forth—Where did I stand today?—was overwhelming. It started to feel so tense to go to school: I couldn't focus in class because I was never sure when I was going to be made fun of, or what was going to happen in the cafeteria, or why the girls around me were passing notes.

Was I the only girl being left out? Of course not. But I didn't see that at the time. I *felt* like I was the only one, because it was so utterly painful to be ostracized—and because no one was talking about it. And rather than wonder why these girls were being so mean, I took it very personally. *What's wrong with me?* I wondered. *Will I ever be liked and included?* In a short period of time, I'd gone from an incredibly confident, outspoken young girl to an insecure, timid sixth grader filled with anxiety. My grades started to drop, and when opportunities came up—to try out for a team or run for class office—I didn't take them, even though I knew I had something to offer. I was too scared the other girls would ridicule me for trying.

Thankfully, the popular-girl drama wasn't the only thing I experienced during middle school. Unwittingly I also started something that would have more of an impact on my future than I could ever know: I enlisted the help of a few adult mentors. Sure, I had my mom to talk to. (And since I know a lot of girls can't talk to their parents, I'm supergrateful to have her unwavering support.) But she was my *mom*—she wasn't in school with me, and she couldn't completely understand what I was going through. I often spent my lunch period in the library to avoid the lunch-room drama, and I started sharing my problems with our school's librarian, Mrs. Lentz. My English teacher, Ms. Presley, also helped me through some rough moments.

But the person I relied on the most was a high school friend I met on my school dance team, Christie. Since she was a few years older than me, she was automatically cooler and more experienced in my eyes—which meant that I respected her and listened to her more than anyone else. (Honestly, I hung on every word she said.) When I went to her with my problems, she told me that she could relate because she had been there too. She had been the butt of jokes in middle school, but she'd gotten through it, and she was positive that I would too. "Forget about them," she'd say. "Let's go to the mall." *Well,* I remember thinking to myself, *If she thinks I'm cool enough to hang out with, then I can't be that bad.* Christie and a few other high school friends—I thought of them as adopted older sisters—fueled me with the inspiration to keep going with my head held high. They were my saving graces, the lifeboats that got me through.

High school has its own unique set of issues, but by the time I started ninth grade, I was out of the roughest waters and I no longer dreaded school each day. But when my little sister started coming home from school in tears, sick from the torment she faced from other girls, I realized it wasn't just me; other middle school girls—maybe even *all* middle school girls—face these same issues. It doesn't have to be this way, I thought: Just because so many girls grow accustomed to being teased or left out or aren't sure who to turn to for help doesn't mean it should continue. I thought about how Christie and my other mentors had understood me more than anyone else, since they'd just been in my shoes—and how I'd found strength from my relationships with them.

Then it hit me: What if we found a way for other tween girls to have the same experience that I had with my older friends? A way for middle school girls to share their troubles openly and honestly in a group, without worrying about being judged? And what if high school girls led the group as mentors? They'd share what worked for them in middle school, what didn't, and what they'd learned. They'd be there to inspire and guide the younger girls. And by sharing in this safe space, the tweens would learn to rely on and trust one another rather than turn on each other. It might even be like an instant sisterhood.

I sketched out details for this new idea, named the group Girl Talk, and lobbied my school administration for approval. Once my incredibly supportive principal, Mr. Henry, signed on, the program was born.

Girl Talk's basic premise is the same now as it was back then. High school girls lead middle school girls in weekly discussion groups about everything from body image issues to having self-respect; from how to deal with mean girls and bullying to the importance of being kind; from meeting guys and dating to getting along with your parents. (Our organization offers the program for free; it trains the leaders and provides themed curricula for each meeting.) The middle school girls get instant adopted big sisters and a safe place to talk openly. The high school girls become real-life role models and are expected to act accordingly. And we emphasize volunteering and service throughout each chapter's community, so every girl involved comes away with greater compassion for and perspective on the world around her.

It's a simple idea that creates a lasting effect. Most of the young girls involved—83 percent—become Girl Talk Leaders when they get to high school. And we've seen that if girls have a substantial outlet to talk about what's going on in their lives, they'll improve their work in the classroom (as I instinctively knew in sixth grade when my grades dropped because of my dismal social situation): we've found a 14 percent improvement in Girl Talk participants' math grades and a 24 percent improvement in language arts grades since they started the program. And of course we've seen positive effects that can't be measured: our Girl Talk Girls and Leaders report feeling more confident and compassionate toward others.

After ten years of running Girl Talk (it's now my full-time job), traveling around the country speaking to groups of middle school girls, and meeting countless adults who parent or work with tweens, I can't tell you how many times a mom, dad, teacher, or counselor has asked for our help. Parents, especially, come to us regularly, saying: "We don't know what to do or say about situation X, Y, or Z. How can we help our girl get through this?" Even with all the information available online and on the shelves of bookstores, they're still confused about their tween girls and are desperate to know how they can help their daughters. As close as you might be to your daughter, you can't walk through the hallways with her, try to find a seat in the cafeteria alongside her, or be with her as she navigates the social dynamics of a Friday night football game.

That's why I wanted to write *The Drama Years*. I'm the head of Girl Talk, not a psychologist or academic, but I'm in this world day in and day out. Girls trust the Girl Talk team. They confide in us and tell us what's *really* happening out there—and this information is too valuable not to share it with you, the parents and adults who work with middle schoolers. In *The Drama Years*, you'll read about a wide range of tween and teen experiences with issues like body image, stress, frenemies, and love.

This information couldn't be more vital. Research has shown that the period between sixth and eighth grades is one of the most critical times in a young person's development: the decisions girls make during these years, and the paths they start to walk down, directly affect and inform the adult they will become. These are the years where peers replace parents and other adults as major influencers. This means that it's crucial for parents and other adults who work with these girls to understand the situations that will inevitably arise in their lives and to hear, direct from the source, how they want the adults around them to handle these changes.

Why name the book *The Drama Years*? Because that's exactly how girls describe their experiences during this time. Fights between friends are "drama"; starting to experience crushes can cause "drama"; middle school in general is "so much drama." While parents might playfully roll their eyes, it's very real to tween girls. They're dramatic; their friends are dramatic. To them, it feels like *life* is dramatic.

What to Expect in *The Drama Years*

In *The Drama Years,* I'll take you through the big issues girls face today. First, we'll look at self-awareness— how tween girls can find out who they are in the midst of all the influences surrounding them. In Chapter 2, you'll see how to help girls tackle stress, a growing problem among tweens, who feel under pressure to be all things to all people. We'll look at materialism and competition around name brands in Chapter 3 and what's *really* underneath that obsession with the latest designer jeans. Linked to the pressure to have the latest name brands is the pressure to look a certain way; that's the focus of Chapter 4, about body image and body awareness. Chapter 5 deals with one of the largest sources of both happiness and devastation for middle school girls: their friends. You'll learn about mean girls, frenemies, and bullying and how to help your tween recognize a good friend. Next, in Chapter 6, we'll look at love relationships and sexuality. Dealing with you—parents and other adults—is the subject of Chapter 7; you'll see why arguments occur between parents and tweens and how to communicate better with your middle schooler. Chapter 8 is about boundaries, rules, and limits, and how other middle school parents are tackling the same issues you are. Finally, in Chapter 9, we'll get to serious topics—the *real* drama— like family problems, depression, and self-harm.

For each of these issues, I've kept to the spirit of Girl Talk, in which girls share their experiences: what they've learned from each other and from their high school leaders. (After all, there's nothing quite as affirming as hearing that you're not alone.) In terms of the topics we'll cover, I've let the girls speak for themselves—they'll tell you what they think you should know.

Writing *The Drama Years* took many hours of in-depth, personal one-on-one interviews with more than fifty tweens, teens, and adults, collecting anecdotes, thoughts, opinions, and suggestions for how girls felt the adults in their lives helped, or could have helped more. (Names of the girls interviewed and some others have been changed.)

These girls are from all over the country, from New York City to small southern towns, from Florida to Washington State. They're a diverse group, but their experiences are remarkably similar—often girls in completely different locations would offer the same idea—giving a realistic, big picture view of what it's like to be a middle school girl today. (To be interviewed for *The Drama Years*, a middle school girl only had to fit the age requirement—eleven through thirteen, or grades 6 through 8—and to have her parents' permission.)

Their anecdotes and questions are incredibly insightful, often funny, and sometimes heartbreaking. Think of their experiences as a chance to (safely) eavesdrop on the tween girl in your life. If you sense your daughter isn't telling you everything anymore, here's your chance to find out what might be going on for her—these girls aren't shy about revealing their experiences!

Not everything you read will surprise you, and *The Drama Years* doesn't encompass everything that girls today are facing. For the purposes of this book, I've mostly stuck to day-to-day struggles—the emotional, social, and psychological realities that underlie your, "How was school today?" conversations. (I leave the extremely serious topics, like eating disorders, abuse, and addiction, to those trained in dealing with them. At the back of the book, you'll find a list of resources for not only the subjects covered in *The Drama Years* but those I don't cover as well.)

These are real girls facing real issues. You might not be shocked by their stories, but I hope you'll gain some insight from their emotional (and sometimes brutal) honesty, and that their thoughts will help you better relate to the middle schooler in your life. I hope you'll see your daughter and her friends reflected in these girls, and you'll finish *The Drama Years* feeling more compassion and a greater understanding for what she's going through. Sometimes all it takes is hearing another eleven-year-old tell her story to help you better realize why *your* eleven-year-old is stressed, or sad, or angry.

Since *The Drama Years* relies on a large community of voices, you won't find definite answers for how to deal with specific situations. Instead, the experts—high school or early-college-age girls who've just been there—offer their advice. In the "High Schoolers Look Back" boxes, they reflect on what they experienced in middle school, what they wished their parents had done to help, and what their parents did do that they respected and valued. In "Just-Been-There Advice," the high schoolers offer suggestions to adults (and to the middle schoolers themselves, for parents to share with their girls). And in "High Schoolers Decode," they interpret middle schoolers' behavior for adults. These high school girls are all part of the huge, nationwide community of Girl Talk Leaders, so they've already had valuable experience serving as a role model to middle school girls and have led younger girls in discussions about these topics. You can trust their voices. These are the girls you'll *want* to learn from, since they're the ones who are passionate about helping their younger peers. (And although they're only a few years older—some are just a year away from the middle school girls we quote—that leap from middle school to high school is monumental in terms of maturity and experience.) The older mentors show that these tweens are not alone in how they feel; they also decode some middle school behavior for you and share how their parents helped, or didn't, as they navigated these same issues.

In each chapter, you'll notice a pattern: after defining the issue from the tweens' perspective, I'll go more deeply into the reasons that these things—body image worries, friend drama—affect girls as much as they do, especially during middle school. Then I'll discuss what adults can do to help the girls in their lives deal with these problems. (I'll offer activities and exercises for you to implement with your tween; you'll see those in the "Try This" boxes.) You'll read more about my own experiences throughout, and you'll see why I'm convinced that there are three overall keys to raising a grounded, stable, and happy middle school girl— three things you can implement in her life today that will prove to be transformative.

I hope that *The Drama Years* will help anyone who lives or works with middle school girls understand and empathize with what it's like to be a tween girl today. But in writing the book, I have an even bigger hope—a secret mission, so to speak.

About five years ago, after a meeting with one of Girl Talk's biggest supporters, Atlanta philanthropist Ron Bell, I asked Ron why he'd chosen Girl Talk to support. "Because women are influencers," he answered. If we can reach girls at this age and help them to become strong, smart, kind women, they'll influence those around them in a positive way. He wasn't just investing in me, he said; he was investing in all the girls reached by Girl Talk and their future impact on the people around them. "I know the influence my mother's had on me and those around her, and I see the influence my wife and daughter have on other people," he said.

That moment stayed with me, because that's when I realized that my mission wasn't just to help the girls who are involved with Girl Talk. It's to help all girls change for the better, for generations to come. I'm convinced that today's tweens can break the mean girl cycle that's dramatically worsened over the past few years. Instead of perpetuating drama throughout college and into adult life, I firmly believe that with the help of great mentors, today's girls can actively choose to develop their own sense of self and not engage in hurtful behavior—to act instead in ways that show respect for themselves and those around them.

By giving you the tools to help empower the tween girls in your life to become more compassionate and understanding young women, this book can plant that seed. After reading *The Drama Years,* I hope you'll be able to influence the middle school girl in your life in a positive way, and I hope you'll know that you're making an investment in girls everywhere when you do.

Because I witness this kind of transformation happening in the girls I work with every day, I don't see a generation of kind, respectful women as a far-off dream. If we start turning the tide now, it'll ultimately become our reality.

CHAPTER ONE

Staying True to Her

Self-Esteem, Self-Awareness, and Self-Respect

"Every girl in this school wants to be someone else."
—Bridget, thirteen, New Jersey

As a little girl, I loved to dance. I started taking ballet lessons when I was three years old and from then on practiced routines for hours in front of the mirrored wall in our living room. Throughout elementary school, I even gave impromptu performances for my parents and their friends. When a new round of classes began each year, I'd race to the store with my mom to buy a new leotard, skirt, and pair of tights.

When the popular girls in my grade started to exclude me—and when I no longer had my best friend, Maryashley, to talk to—dance became even more essential. For me, it wasn't just a hobby or a form of exercise; it was my lifeline. I signed up for three classes a week and practiced for two hours a day. When I danced, I went into the zone: I forgot about whatever mean thing had been said to me that day or the weekend sleepover that I hadn't been invited to. Only a few girls from my school were in those classes, so I didn't feel as if I was under that same microscope. Plus, all the girls were at different levels of experience, and we were all there because we loved to dance. I wasn't the best dancer at my studio, but I did feel at home there. I knew what I was doing and felt confident in my abilities.

But sometime around seventh grade, all of this changed. I didn't try as hard to excel: I was suddenly scared of falling and being perceived as a klutz. They used to place me in the front row during recitals, but now I was put in the middle, or the back, because I wasn't shining as much during class as I had. And the worst part was that I felt relieved at that change: if I didn't try to get back on top, then I wouldn't be in the spotlight.

Now, as an adult, I see what was going on. My insecurity at school among the girls in my grade had touched other parts of my life. I wasn't trying as hard because I didn't want to be noticed; I didn't want to be judged by the girls in my dance class in the same way that my classmates criticized me. There was less pressure, less attention, less drama that way.

That intense self-consciousness held me back—and I know now that it holds back other girls too. Girls who might want to try out for the soccer team or debate club might second-guess that urge out of a fear of being ridiculed or stereotyped.

Many tween girls feel the same way I did: they just want to blend in without attracting attention because they're so worried they'll be scrutinized or made fun of. Since *everyone's* feeling insecure, it becomes especially easy to criticize others; they're just hoping to deflect any potential teasing.

Middle schoolers are faced with overwhelming changes—biological, hormonal, social, emotional—in a very short period of time, culminating in a perfect storm of self-consciousness. Without knowing how to handle all these new issues, they find it easy to target others in an attempt to stave off that underlying anxiety.

This is why the three years between sixth and eighth grade are an incredibly fragile period, and why it's vitally important for a girl to have a strong sense of self before she enters middle school. If your tween girl isn't aware of who she is and what she's about, she won't have the confidence to try new things, take risks, or take a stand—no matter what anyone says.

Given all this, it's understandable why girls so often base their sense of self on how other people see them. What does *self-esteem* mean? Here's what our tween girls said:

"When I think of self-esteem, I think of if you feel good about yourself, or if you let people tease you. A lot of girls think they're ugly. They're so hard on themselves. I think a lot of girls don't like the way they're made."

—Emma, twelve, New Jersey

"Self-esteem is how you see yourself. It has a lot to do with how others see you, and if you take that in or not, and a lot of people do take that in."

—Kelly, thirteen, New Jersey

Every girl answered with a version of the same idea: that self-esteem is all about what *other* people think and how that affects her opinion of herself—not how she sees herself regardless of the opinions of others. Most of our girls didn't feel that they knew their core self, that solid ground of their personality that was exclusively them. They didn't mention their families, their grades, their love of sports or music or other after-school activities, their connection to their religion, or even their general feelings about who they were on the inside. Instead, their self-esteem depended on where they fell on the social ladder and whether they were victims of teasing (factors that can change daily, even instantly).

If girls' confidence in middle school is based on how their peers see them at any given moment, then it's no wonder that it drops drastically during this time when everyone's social status becomes unstable. It's something psychologists, researchers, and writers began to tell parents in the mid-1990s, when a host of books about girls' self-esteem, like Mary Pipher's *Reviving Ophelia* and Peggy Orenstein's *Schoolgirls*, appeared on bookshelves across the country. These researchers found that girls who were curious, confident, and brimming with enthusiasm and zest for life in grade school often morphed into introverted, insecure middle schoolers. Their test scores dropped, and where they once were the first to answer questions in class, they now hardly raised their hands.

Pamela, mother of a middle school girl, describes watching this transformation in her daughter. "The confidence drop happens overnight," she says. "A lot of it has to do with this expectation of how they're supposed to act. Over the summer, so many of her friends were getting ready for middle school, changing everything about themselves. When she started school, it was like you could almost watch her shoulders hunching, her head drop down. She wasn't a victim of bullying, but it wasn't safe, like elementary school."

Why does this happen? Twelve-year-old New Jersey

native Emma offers this explanation: "In fourth grade, you don't think about yourself too much," she says. But in sixth grade, girls *do* think about themselves . . . all the time. And the comparisons start in earnest; they're wondering, *Am I pretty enough, smart enough, cool enough—for my friends, for the popular group, for the guys?* Rebecca, a thirteen-year-old Texan, is brutally honest about how her insecurities drive her to think about whether she needs to somehow "fix" herself to be accepted: "I'd like to know how I look through other people's eyes," she says. "Sometimes when I have quiet moments, I start thinking bad things, like, 'What if I'm not right? What if something is wrong with me? What do I need to do to change myself?' I'll make a new playlist on my iTunes to make me feel cooler. I'll go through my whole room and change everything. I'll go to the bathroom and give myself a new makeup look."

Your tween girl's social sphere now matters a million times more than it did in elementary school. So every decision she makes, no matter how trivial, often needs to pass a peer-approval process, similar to what Rebecca noted. At the same time, the teasing has ramped up—many girls talk about how hard it is to avoid the cruelty from other girls or from guys—so they're spending a lot of psychic energy just trying to avoid embarrassing comments from their peers (who are, as we mentioned earlier, all too quick to repress and stave off their own insecurity by attacking others). "It's pretty difficult to keep your self-esteem up," says Valerie, a twelve-year-old in Michigan. "Just the other day a boy in my class told me I was ugly, right to my face."

What's the major way that girls try to deal with these pressures? From what they tell us—and it's something every parent or teacher of tween girls knows—they'll do it by conforming and trying to fit in. But that's not a process girls are blindly going through. They're not just trying to instantaneously morph into an Everygirl who can magically avoid all teasing and who will always win the support of her peers. They *know* they're changing to please others, and not everyone's okay with that. For many of them, it's a supremely uncomfortable line to walk, but they're not sure what to do instead. Charlotte and Emma are walking that exact tightrope—they're torn between wanting to be true to themselves and wanting to fit in with their classmates:

"It's hard to just be myself. I don't want to fit in 100 percent and end up wearing what everyone is wearing, but I don't want to stand out a lot of the time, because then you'll feel weird for being totally different."

—Charlotte, twelve, California

"When I first got to middle school, my friends and I split up, because they started wearing makeup, and I wasn't wearing makeup yet. When I was twelve, my mom let me wear makeup, and people started liking me. I didn't feel like myself, but I made more friends. I was acting fake, but it helped me through the first half of my middle school year. I wish that I could relax and be completely myself. I want people to like me for who I am—but at the same time, I don't want to get made fun of."

—Emma, twelve, New Jersey

The girl who stays true to herself through it all, who can do exactly what she wants to do, whether it's socially acceptable or not, is rare, says Kris, a middle school counselor. "It all depends on the girl: The more power she thinks she has, the more she can do what she wants. If she feels confident enough to say, 'I'm done with dance class because I really want to play ultimate Frisbee,' it would be an interesting move. But it would really depend on the rest of her friends deciding together, 'Is that the cool thing to do, or should we ostracize her?'"

When I started middle school, I wasn't the strong kind of girl that Kris describes. Thanks to the intensity of that assumed spotlight, that feeling that *everyone* was watching and judging me, I transformed from an ultraconfident opinionated fifth grader to a quiet wallflower. And that change was all about the others around me—just like in dance class. I wanted the approval of the popular girls, but without pandering to or sucking up to them, so I just tried to get by unnoticed. I wanted to be a cheerleader, but I was too scared that I'd mess up the tumbling to try out. I wanted to run for student council, but I was worried that someone would say, "I can't believe *she* thinks she can win." I turned inward in order to stay under the radar—to *not* shine because I didn't want to give other girls more reason to talk about me. I knew my fear was holding me back. But at the time, it felt like a matter of social survival.

And this is what many girls say their parents just don't understand, even with the best of intentions. "I think they *want* to understand it, but I don't think they ever will," says Emma. "They won't ever be in my shoes, walking through the hallway and being called ugly. They could never realize what I'm going through in middle school."

In interviews with both tweens and their parents, a few things stood out. Most parents said they want to help their daughters keep a strong sense of self throughout these years, but many are too busy to spend a lot of time helping their daughters on that journey of self-discovery—or they don't know just how important it is. Ann, who had good intentions to save her daughter from possible ridicule, ended up inadvertently shutting down her self-expression:

> *"Sometimes my daughter will wear an outfit that will have me asking, 'What were you thinking?' The other morning I said, 'You need to go upstairs and change.' She said, 'I think I look great!' And without thinking, I said, 'You look like a train wreck!' Her eyes started welling up with tears, and I felt guilty, but on the other hand, as a mother, I thought, I'm not letting her leave the house like that, because she'll get teased for it in school. I tried to explain later, and she said, 'You could've been nicer.' I said, 'You know what? You're going to go out into the world and not everyone's going to be nice.'"*
>
> —Ann, middle school mom

To parents trying to juggle work, kids, and their own lives, all the middle school drama can seem to be just that: drama. After all, as Ann says, girls need to know how to deal with conflict in the adult world, right? Of course. But while there may be backstabbing and gossip at your office or workplace, or among a group of friends, when was the last time someone walked up to you and pointed out to everyone, in the cruelest way possible, the *one* flaw you've been desperately trying to hide? *That's* middle school.

It's not easy to know how to respond to every situation, especially when you're dealing with a host of adult concerns of your own that your tween knows nothing about. Parents trying to navigate these waters often feel scared, frustrated, and impatient, as well as worry that time is running out to make sure their daughter is equipped with all she needs. "You have a really small window when they're going downhill to rein them back in," says Pamela, a middle school mom. Another middle school mom, Kathy, reports a similar feeling of fear of losing control: "It's devastating to hear about my daughter being made fun of. It's hard to not immediately respond back. My husband and I try to say, 'Okay, I know you want to talk, but do you want to vent? Do you want advice?' What's she looking for? But it's so hard to stop and not react. We are constantly watching to make sure it doesn't turn into something worse—that it doesn't turn into depression or going down some other road and using substances. It's always on your mind."

So what can parents do to help their daughters feel surer of themselves? Here's what our middle school girls said helped them:

- **Express empathy.**
"Parents should just listen to their daughters and really hear them out about what's going on in middle school. When you know that your parents are there for you, it makes it so much easier to understand that you can do it, you can get through this."

—Emma, twelve, New Jersey

- **Share your experience.**
"My mom was the least popular girl in her grade. So even when we have disagreements and arguments, I still know she understands what I'm going through, because in a lot of ways, she had it even worse. She's told me, 'It doesn't matter what they think about you; it only matters what you think about yourself, and it's important

that you know you're a strong person, and you have to make sure the friends you choose for life are true friends who will always be there for you.'"

—Valerie, twelve, Michigan

- ## Distract her with kindness.
  "Just the other day, my mom took me shopping for a dress for a bat mitzvah, and she picked out a perfect dress and said 'This will make you look gorgeous.' She made me feel really good about myself."

  —Emma, twelve, New Jersey

How else do girls find, and keep, that strong sense of self? Part of it takes practice: girls report that when they do take a leap and stick to what they know is true, they feel stronger—and they understand that it will be easier next time.

Sara, a seventh grader in Florida, says that her self-esteem was the lowest when her group of friends started to ostracize her at lunch. She was able to muster up the inner strength to make a decision on her own for how to proceed; taking that risk and having it pay off is something she'll be able to expand on the next time she feels uncertain:

"Those few weeks when I didn't know why they weren't talking to me, why they were purposefully filling up the lunch table before I came, were the worst. They'd say to each other, 'Remember last Saturday when we went to the mall together? Wasn't that great? Have you used your new perfume?' Except I hadn't gotten the invitation. It was like, 'Wow, they've always liked me. What did I do?' I needed to tell somebody about it, so I talked to my mom. She told

me not to say anything, not to make a huge deal of it. It helped. She didn't baby me and say, 'Oh, this is terrible!!' She knew inside that it was terrible. But when people say, 'Oh, this is awful! I think this is what you should do,' it bothers me. Finally, I just left and went to a different lunch table. I came to the decision to change tables myself and not to say anything mean to the first group. I just kept it quiet. And when I went to sit with these other people, I felt a lot stronger. Now they're my really good friends."

Just-Been-There Advice: What Are You Good At?

"I tell girls that there are people who are always going to be better and going to think they're better than you are, but each person individually brings something to the table. Girls have to cultivate what they're good at: *I* can't play the piano, but maybe your middle school girl is a great piano player. I've learned to stand out in different ways, even if it's being funny or goofy, or taking a leadership role that I was scared to take. I've learned to do that, and it's helped my light shine."

—Ellie, twenty

Taylor, a twelve-year-old from New York, has a similar story of how she changed her situation when she could no longer be herself around her group of friends:

"Last year when I started middle school, there was a group of girls that I was sort of friendly with. I was always trying to get in on their jokes and what they were talking about, and try to hang out with them because they were popular. Sometimes I'd feel okay around them, but sometimes they'd talk about other people and gossip a lot more than I would, and I wasn't really that interested in that gossip. It made me uncomfortable. I was worried they were going to realize I didn't know as much as they did and they would make fun of me. They would call boys at sleepovers and ask who they liked best. I'd be like, What?! That's when I felt awkward and unsure. Sometimes when I was hanging out with those other girls, I felt like I wasn't really being myself. I didn't feel like I was me. It felt like I was kind of pretending. The things they were very interested in just didn't appeal to me. They seemed to have matured faster than I had; it seemed like suddenly, on a dime, they'd gotten a lot older than I had over the summer. I didn't feel like I was ready for that.

"But I was involved with dance and acting at the time, so I had these other places where I could be myself and feel okay. They were kind of outlets because I made friends in this play I was involved in, and I had dance almost every day, so a lot of my other activities and other friends helped me, and that's when I felt like I was totally being myself. That old group and I grew apart, and I was okay with it. I love the people I hang out with now."

Dance and acting were outlets for Taylor, where she could be herself and "feel okay." That's exactly how I felt about my classes too—until seventh grade, when I started semiconsciously holding myself back.

By the middle of my eighth grade year, though, I'd started

working harder, partly because I was now taking private tap lessons out of town, at a studio where I met my new best friend, Lanier. But I was still feeling alone at school. Since I never knew if I'd be left out in the lunchroom, I brought my lunch from home and ate in one of the girls' bathrooms just to avoid the drama. It didn't feel like a big deal to me; it was just a simple way to sidestep the mean girls in the cafeteria. Afterward I'd stop into the library, where I'd hang out with Mrs. Lentz.

On my birthday that year in late April, I was eating lunch in the bathroom as usual when I heard my mom's voice: "Haley?"

Girls Talk: What Makes You Feel Good about Yourself?

- Doing girl stuff, like shopping or seeing a movie, with a parent, an older sister, a mentor, or another adult
- A physical or creative activity that's supported by parents, like horseback riding, dance, soccer, or theater
- Solid relationships with friends who aren't obsessed with social status and popularity
- Making friends outside school, giving her an opportunity to be herself without worrying about repercussions in the hallways
- Compliments from parents and other family members

Why was my mom at school? And how did she know where I was? I hadn't told her that I often ate in the bathroom. "Yes?" I called back as I opened the door of the stall and saw my mom standing before me with a surprised look on her face. "What are you doing in here?" she asked. "Are you okay?" I saw that she was holding a cookie cake (my favorite!)—a birthday surprise for me. When she saw my bagged lunch in my hand, she broke out in tears, and then *I* started crying too. She took me home, and I told her everything. She had known that I was unhappy at school because of the girls in my class, and she knew that I often came home with hurt feelings, but she hadn't known until that moment how bad it was.

Then she proposed a crazy idea. "Why don't you try out for the high school dance team?" she asked me.

"Are you kidding?!" Even though I really, *really* wanted to be on the dance team that next year when I started high school, I didn't see why I should put myself in the spotlight like that. But my mother explained that it'd be a good opportunity to meet new people and put my energy toward moving on to high school.

For the next few weeks, I turned it over and over in my mind: Was I good enough to make it? Did I believe in myself enough to risk the social repercussions of going for it—and possibly not succeeding? Then I had an aha! moment: *What do I have to lose?* I thought. *I'm not gaining anything by not auditioning. But those other girls are just winning: I'm conforming to everything they want me to be.*

Almost immediately after I signed up, the girls in my class started in on me: "Oh, are you nervous about trying out?" they'd ask pointedly. I worked hard to ignore them, and I spent every afternoon with my boom box out under the carport, practicing my routine. Somewhere along the way, attempting to make the team became much bigger than just making the cut; it was my way of proving to myself that I wouldn't let anyone hold me back.

When my mom asked me about tryouts in the car on the way home after them, I told her that I wasn't sure how I did—but I was really proud of myself for going through with it. Even though I knew all those girls doubted me, I thought I'd performed okay. And a few days later, I felt totally overwhelmed when we got the call that I'd made the team. I was superexcited and proud and nervous all at the same time—*and* mostly so relieved that I had stayed true to myself in the first place. I'd stayed committed to something I loved doing and hadn't let the mean girls in my class hold me back.

Christie was on that dance team, and that's where I discovered how powerful and healing it is to have an older girlfriend to serve as a mentor, to tell me that she'd dealt with the same things I was going through. My friendship with Christie and a few of the older girls gave me the confidence to think I could actually make a difference when my younger sister started middle school. My survival throughout these years was due to more than just having Christie as my mentor. During that time, I'd unknowingly merged three things that I honestly think helped me become the person I am now, and these are essential parts of the message we at Girl Talk send to girls and parents:

Three Takeaways to Downplay the Drama

1. An anchor activity
2. A helping hand
3. An adopted older sister

These are also the three things I emphasize throughout this book. Having these in place in a middle schooler's life will not only help her keep her mind off the drama, but they'll serve as a base where she can take refuge when things get tough. Each is invaluable, and when they're used in tandem, they can be transformative.

How do I know this? Again, I'm not an adolescent psychologist, so I can't point to a heap of academic studies as evidence. I know that these three things work because I saw them work in my own life and in the lives of so many girls I've known over the ten years since I started Girl Talk. They just make sense.

You could even implement these as experiments. After a year with these three takeaways to downplay the drama in her life, is your tween girl happier, more stable, and stronger emotionally? I can almost guarantee that she will be. When these factors are in play, she has an outlet to keep her mind off the ups and downs of middle school; she has an opportunity to be of service, to gain some perspective about what's really drama and what's not; and she has someone to decipher and decode her experiences, to let her know that she's not alone:

1. An anchor activity. This could be playing a sport or a musical instrument, participating in theater or a school club, taking art classes, babysitting, or engaging in environmental activism, for instance. As long as it's something that:

- she actively enjoys (not something that *you* enjoy or would just like her to be good at)
- keeps her engaged and she can throw herself into fully

- takes place outside school, so she can be free from the regular social pressures
- seems to fulfill her creatively, intellectually, and socially

We've already talked about the self-consciousness that characterizes the middle school years—how it's often the time when girls feel so insecure about trying something new for fear they'll be ridiculed. But this is precisely the time when they *should* be trying new things. You never know what will become a lifetime hobby or passion. (Think about all the adults you know who wished they'd tried out for that school play or started playing an instrument or a sport when they'd had the chance.)

I've told you how much my dance classes shaped me and how they served as an escape, an activity I could really pour myself into. But they were also a distraction, and in the best possible way. They took up so much time that I wasn't really able to obsess about the drama at school. I'd go to school, go to dance, and come home with just enough time to do homework, eat dinner, and fall into bed. And since it was a form of exercise—and a fun one too—I often felt recharged after my classes.

2. A helping hand. This is a chance for your tween to be a part of something larger than herself, to connect to the community, to instill gratitude for what she has, and to allow her to see the reality of the lives of others. It could be a weekly or monthly volunteer commitment, but the emotional gains that volunteering offers are so much deeper if it's a regular priority in her life—not just a one-time Saturday afternoon activity.

At Girl Talk, we require both our girls and leaders to spend a certain number of hours volunteering, and we've found that they often far exceed the minimum requirement. Volunteering is contagious; when you offer help, you really see that you can make a difference, and you want to keep doing it. Plus, the psychological payoff is incredible. (Science has shown that giving to others is a surefire way toward personal happiness.) So many parents complain that their middle schooler sees herself as the center of the world; here's a chance to short-circuit that immediately and let her see that her daily drama in middle school is only a drop in the bucket.

And like the anchor activity, you never know what might move from a volunteer commitment to a life passion. Former leaders have reported that the service component of Girl Talk led them to find their career path, and they realized that they love working with animals or veterans, or they're now driven to join the Peace Corps.

For me, my mom prompted my helping hand activity. At the beginning of my sixth-grade year, she had developed an eye disease, and by the end of seventh grade, her vision had gone so far downhill that she was eligible to participate in a medical case study, for which she was given a new pair of eyeglasses every ninety days. We would drop off her old glasses at the Lions Literacy Center, a local organization for people with both vision and literacy challenges.

One time, when we were at Lions, I saw a woman waiting in line to be helped. She looked to be in her twenties, and she was crying. When I asked her what was wrong, she told me that she was at the literacy center because she couldn't read, and it was affecting her kindergartner's education. She couldn't introduce him to books or look over his schoolwork. And she knew this was just the beginning; as he went through school, it would get so much worse.

I was taken aback. People in my community didn't know how to read? Really? Her name was Amanda, and I decided right then and there that I wanted to help her. If she could read, she'd be a better mom to her son, get a better job, and provide a better life for her family. The center agreed that I could help.

So I asked my English teacher, Ms. Presley, to help me teach Amanda how to read, and for the next three years, I went to the literacy center once a week after school and worked with Amanda on her reading skills. Not only was it amazing to see the ways in which she started to change her life and to know that I could actually help someone— but I had found a close friend. Working with Amanda put my seventh-grade drama into serious perspective. Whenever I felt down or worried about what someone was going to think of me, I'd remember what Amanda was dealing with and realized how silly my problems would seem to her.

Just like my dance class and my relationship with Christie, I really believe that working with Amanda changed everything for me: I had more confidence, and I felt that I could make a change in the world—I could really help someone and make a difference. Trying to befriend the girls in my class seemed less important.

3. An adopted older sister. This is a positive role model that your middle school girl can look up to. It should be someone who has just been in your girl's shoes and can both relate to her, so she doesn't feel as alone, and advise her on how to handle whatever she's going through.

My relationship with Christie was a lifesaver. And now that I have spent a decade running an organization focused on mentoring, I've seen countless girls go from not only surviving but thriving in middle school—thanks to the support and confidence boosters they've received from adopted older sisters. Girls feel comforted by the knowledge that they aren't the only ones who didn't get invited to every sleepover or felt insecure about their looks, or had parents who split up—and they're hearing it from an older (and therefore cooler!) girl they can emulate and learn from. When they're having a bad day, girls can text, Skype, or Gchat their slightly older friends and get advice—and take heart in the fact that even if their friends don't think they're amazing, a high schooler does.

These three takeaways to downplay the drama are invaluable ways to help your tween discover who she really is. By immersing herself in an anchor activity, lending a helping hand to a cause she believes in, and creating a strong relationship with an adopted older sister, she'll develop incredibly rich values that will form her core—the part of herself that's truly her and won't get swayed when things get tough. She'll learn what gets her excited, optimistic, and curious about life, and she'll realize the power of commitment and compassion.

Besides serving as a home base for your tween, these ways to downplay the drama will also help her counteract the stresses and anxieties of daily life. And believe me, there are many, many things that are stressing out today's girls—as we'll discover in the next chapter.

Try This: Help Her Find Her True Self

- **Create self-image self-portraits.** Ask your middle schooler to draw a self-portrait. On half of the page, ask her to draw how she sees herself, and on the other half, have her portray how she thinks the world sees her. If she's a verbal learner instead of a visual one, have her list adjectives that she'd use to describe herself on one side of the page, and on the other, ask her to list the words others would use to describe her. Together, discuss the images she drew or the words she listed.

- **Start a confidence team.** Each morning on her bathroom mirror, use a dry erase marker to write three things that make her beautiful on the inside: her wit, her tenacity, her willingness to help around the house, for example. Ask her to do the same for you—it's a self-esteem booster for you both.

- **Plan a self-esteem scavenger hunt.** Leave books, quotes, and pictures that remind her of how awesome she truly is. She'll feel confident and loved, and your understanding will build a stronger relationship between you both.

- **Just for you: Walk the walk.** Remember that your tween models her behavior on the adults around her. Are there obvious ways that you're not being true to yourself? Is your own self-esteem lacking? It's important to make sure that you're not just supporting her, but that you're a strong self-esteem role model too.

The Bottom Line

- Middle school girls often see themselves through the eyes of others and aren't sure yet who they truly are.

- Since their sense of self is subject to change so rapidly, it's common to see major decreases in self-esteem once girls start middle school.

- Tweens feel conflicted and equally torn between staying true to themselves and fitting in.

- Parents can offer three life-changing ways to help tween girls that will help girls discover who they truly are and weather many of the ups and downs of middle school:
  - An **anchor activity**—an outside-school activity that she can throw herself into
  - A **helping hand**—an ongoing commitment to volunteer at an organization that she feels passionate about
  - An **adopted older sister**—a stable role model that she can trust and confide in

CHAPTER TWO

I'm So Stressed!
Handling Everyday Anxiety

"Stress is when everything comes together at a point—everything you've been worrying about, everything you have to do—and you realize 'This isn't working.' And then you freak out."

—Haley, twelve, Washington

Getting ready for school every day when I was a tween was never just about making sure I had all my books and homework. Countless worries and anxieties swirled through my mind each morning. *What should I wear? Will my friends like me today? Am I going to be invited to the sleepover on Friday? Am I good enough for these girls? Will I always feel this left out?* And this is all while juggling tons of schoolwork and dealing with a body that was changing and growing on a daily basis.

One afternoon in sixth grade, it all came to a head: my little brother was picking on me (it was something so trivial I can't even remember what it was), and I burst into tears and ran to my room. I felt overwhelmed by all of these anxieties. I didn't know it at the time, but there was a name for what I was going through: stress.

Parents might think stress is a grown-up problem, but I certainly wasn't the only middle schooler experiencing incredible anxiety then. Sure, these girls aren't dealing with mortgages, demanding bosses, personal businesses, families, and households, but still: middle-school girls know what it means to be stressed out. Here's how they define it:

"Stress is when you have something that's worrying you, and you can't get over it. It's hanging on to you."
—Tabitha, eleven, New York

"It's when you're feeling overwhelmed with everything around you that's happening in your life; it gets hard and you get frustrated. It's like your mind is blowing up."
—Fiona, twelve, Virginia

Adults might not even be aware that their middle schooler is feeling this way. Given all the grown-up anxiety in the world today, it can be easy for adults to overlook or downplay the stress their middle school girls are experiencing— or forget that their girls understand stress in the first place. "'What do kids have to be stressed about?' That's what parents think," says Leni, a middle school mom in New York City. Elena, a thirteen-year-old in Washington State, gets a similar reaction from her mom:

"If I say I'm stressed out, she says 'You're too young to be stressed.' Maybe that was true when I was in fifth grade,

but now there are more expectations. I'm afraid if I talk to her about it that it won't get anywhere. She'll say, 'There's nothing to be stressed about.' But just because I have my whole life to be stressed doesn't mean I'm not stressed now."

In fact, a 2009 study from the American Psychological Association found that 26 percent of middle schoolers felt more stressed than they had the prior year—but only 17 percent of parents thought their child's stress had increased. Maybe Leni, the New York mom, has a key to understanding that disparity: she noticed that her middle schooler doesn't use adult vocabulary to identify her feelings, which might make it harder to identify what's really wrong. "She calls it 'nervous' or 'upset,'" she says. "They have other ways of describing stress, and as adults, we just call it 'stress.' Parents don't always pick up on these verbal cues."

What's the Pressure About—and Who's Pressuring Them?

Why are these girls dealing with so much anxiety at such a young age? Here's what girls tell me stresses them out:

- **Keeping up with school**
  "Every year it gets harder; I could be up until 11:30 every night doing homework."
  —Jessica, thirteen, New Jersey

- **Negotiating friend issues**
  "My year was going really well, and then all my friends turned on me. They weren't being truthful to me, and

that got me stressed: for a month, I was crying because I was just worried that no one liked me anymore."

—Hayley, twelve, Washington

• **Balancing all their activities**

"I used to dance every afternoon after school, but I had to quit. I'd go to sleep at midnight and wake up at six. Doing that five times a week—it started to stress me out."

—Sara, twelve, Florida

• **All of the above**

"Grades, volleyball, friend drama. I'm pretty stressed out on a daily basis."

—Rebecca, thirteen, Texas

These reasons for anxiety are both external, like juggling all their activities, and internal, like the increasing pressure that comes with negotiating friend drama and balancing extreme societal expectations to be "perfect." A normal tween girl's daily schedule—like Erica's—could overwhelm even the most calm and collected among us:

"Right after school I try to work on my homework as much as I can before my mom picks me up. Then I'm at dance for three hours. Then I try to do my homework on the way home. During the week I don't have time for TV, friends, the Internet. Saturday is the only day I can do that. On Sunday I'm doing homework for most of the day."

—Erica, twelve, Georgia

At thirteen, Florida native Max sounds like a woman three times her age when she talks about juggling her academic and after-school to-do list: "I feel like some kind of a superhuman managing all of this stuff."

It's not surprising that our high schoolers recalled feeling stressed out almost as soon as they started middle school; for years now, girls have reported increasing levels of stress during this time. When *Seventeen* magazine conducted a major survey in 2005 in conjunction with Johns Hopkins University, it found that 99 percent of its more than 1,000 respondents felt stressed, and 35 percent thought they had

High Schoolers Look Back: We Dealt with It Too

"In middle school, one of my biggest fears and stressors was disappointing my parents."

—Kimmi, sixteen

"The combination of having to make good grades, trying to impress my teachers and parents, and swimming—it was really hard, time management-wise."

—Britney, sixteen

"The girls in my class stressed me out. I was new in seventh grade, and my school was much bigger and the people were much different; the girls had experienced so much more. I had to get used to that."

—Haven, sixteen

to be "perfect." And in a survey of 3,000 middle school and high school students, psychologist Dr. Roni Cohen-Sandler, author of *Stressed-Out Girls: Helping Them Thrive in the Age of Pressure,* found that at this age, girls experience much more school-related stress than boys do, precisely because they want to be the best. More than two-thirds of her middle school girl respondents said they "usually" or "always" pressure themselves to succeed. The girls I talk to often echo that desire to avoid mistakes at all costs, like Kaitlin, a thirteen-year-old in Georgia: "It seems like every second of every day, I'm always trying to be my best. If I even mess up once, I'm harder on myself than other people are on me."

And it can become even more intense, with feelings that their entire future is at stake. "There's a lot of responsibility in eighth grade," says Jessica, a thirteen-year-old in New Jersey. "It can get very overwhelming. And there's a lot of pressure to do good so I can do good in high school. Your future rests on what you're doing now. Every time I get a test back, it's impacting my life."

For eleven-year-old Kalli in Florida, her entire identity rests on being the perfect student: "I'm known for getting straight As and being the best reader. If I didn't do well in school, I'd have nothing."

So who's putting all this pressure on girls today? It would be easy to blame the teachers for giving homework, or the parents for overscheduling, or the mean girls for, well, being mean. But tweens feel it's a combination—it's not just coming from one source, as you'll see below:

- **They feel pressure from inside: they're criticizing themselves when things go wrong, they're making comparisons to their friends, and they're constantly striving to be better.**

"I want to be perfect, but I know I'm not going to get there."

—Erin, thirteen, Georgia

"If something goes wrong in a friendship, I blame myself. I've lost a lot of friends and haven't been able to figure out why, so I usually suspect I must've done something."

—Hayley, twelve, Washington

- **They feel pressure from their parents, especially to do well in school; they think that everything that happens in their lives now counts for their future.**

  "My parents say education is really important so I don't end up without a job. If I mess up, I think, 'What is this going to start in me? I'll flunk out of eighth grade, and then I'll never be able to do the things I want to do.'"

  —Hillary, thirteen, Georgia

- **They feel pressure from society at large to conform to the standard perceptions of "nice" girls–to be perpetually happy and cheerful, even when they don't want to be.**

  "Everyone who knows me is like, 'Oh, she's never mean, she's so nice.' But sometimes it comes to that point where you can't take it anymore and you want to explode."

  —Kelly, thirteen, New Jersey

Although girls understand it as a combination of factors, when pressed, they will usually blame only one person for the pressure they're under: themselves.

I totally get that fear of failure—that unspoken, underlying worry that they won't be as liked, or as loved, or as accepted if they're not always "perfect." I was guilty of this throughout middle school too. I set incredibly high expectations for myself and those around me, and I felt like any misstep, no matter how small, would be a grave disappointment to my parents, or that if I made one wrong move, the bottom would fall out from beneath me.

But trial and error is how we learn. I once heard a female executive speak about "failing forward," and it stayed with me. Now I think of my mistakes through that failing-forward lens, saying to myself, "Okay, I've stumbled, but what can I learn from this situation?" It took me a long time to realize this, but it's been so transformative for me that I hope it's something that girls and parents can practice too.

For instance, part of my job at Girl Talk is to speak to large groups of people about our organization. When I started making these presentations, I'd breeze through the story of how Girl Talk was born. I didn't want to spend too much time talking about it because I didn't want people to think that it was all about me and my experience, since so many people have been integral to the success of Girl Talk. Later, I wondered why the presentation didn't translate into new chapter growth.

This happened a few times before a mentor of mine pulled me aside and said, "You know, you're speeding through the Girl Talk story so quickly that the audience doesn't really *get* it. You're not clearly explaining what the organization does and what purpose it serves."

Well, of course, this made me feel like a *giant* failure. By not clearly articulating our mission, I had probably missed out on helping a ton of girls just out of fear of sounding as if I was boasting. I spent a while beating myself up about it before I realized that this was actually a great opportunity to learn. If I wanted to succeed, I'd have to find a way to stop wasting energy getting angry at myself for "failing" and learn how I could improve from these experiences. *Okay,* I said to myself. *How can I do a better job at my next presentation?* That's what I mean by "failing forward." Since my realization, having a more positive, active reaction to my mistakes has been a huge help for overcoming my perfectionist tendencies.

But during middle school, I wasn't able to think of my mistakes in that way just yet. And like most other middle school girls, at the time I couldn't distinguish between an actual stressful situation and one that I should shrug off. Was decorating my locker stressful? It shouldn't have been. But figuring out which were the cool magnets (versus the ones that might inspire cruel jokes) *felt* just as stressful as making straight A's, which in turn was just as stressful as stepping up my responsibilities at home to help my mom as she dealt with possibly losing her vision. I was equally stressed about having the coolest backpack and asking my dad for lunch money when our finances were tight. It was all one big knot in my stomach.

Over the years, I've talked to many girls with serious problems at home—a mom with breast cancer, a dad who's just been laid off—and they've had the same trouble distinguishing between stressors and compartmentalizing stress. Adults will tell me that the girls in their lives have no idea what they're dealing with behind the scenes. They'll say that they're trying to figure out how to pay medical bills, or get a new job, or take care of aging parents. And that's all true, but those are adult stressors. Girls have their own.

Audrey, one of our sixteen-year-old high schoolers, had this same problem until she started to have stress-related digestive issues in middle school. Getting sick, she said, was an unforeseen gift because it forced her to start putting

Girls Talk:
How Do You React to Stress?

- Feeling easily overwhelmed
- Feeling anxious
- Worrying
- Suffering from headaches
- Unable to sleep
- Crying
- Uncontrollable anger
- Digestive problems

"My mind races a lot. Sometimes I can't sleep because I'm just thinking so much."

—Erica, twelve, Georgia

"If I'm doing homework and it's 11:00 P.M. and I know I should be asleep, I'll get really worked up and anxious and start crying because there's so much pressure."

—Elena, thirteen, Washington

"Life comes rushing quickly, and I freak out. My mind kind of stops, and I don't feel good about anything. All my confidence, everything that's *me* leaves me, so I'm this blank circle."

—Hayley, twelve, Washington

"Sometimes my body just starts shaking."

—Kelly, thirteen, New Jersey

things in perspective. "Nothing in life is worth your health," she says. "Girls have to decide what's worth stressing about. Are they stressed out because their shirt doesn't match their shoes, or because something really serious has happened? Thinking that way helped me to limit the drama; there wasn't so much, 'She didn't say hi to me, so I'm mad at her.'"

Sure, some stress is good. "I think that fear of growing up and being nothing is a motivator," says thirteen-year-old Hillary, "and you need to build a strong root so the tree won't fall down." But while Audrey's example is an extreme one, more often than not our girls have reported that stress takes a real toll on their bodies, minds, and spirits. Not surprisingly, the American Psychological Association study I mentioned earlier found alarming increases in stress-related physical problems like headaches, sleeplessness, and over- or undereating in preteens.

Racing minds, crying, lost sleep. Should girls this age really be dealing with this much stress? "A thirteen-year-old girl shouldn't be so stressed out and anxious that she's having panic attacks," says eighteen-year-old Grace, one of the high schoolers we interviewed. She's right.

So how can you help the girl in your life? When it comes to your role in your tween girl's stress, it can be hard to know where to draw the line. It really does matter whether she tries her best in school, but how do you know when you're pushing too hard? On the next page, high schoolers give their thoughts.

I'd add another tip to the high schoolers' list: try to be a support for your tween girl. They're feeling so much pressure that they say things that you know are unfounded, like, "If I don't pass this test, I won't get into college!" *You* know that getting a B on a seventh-grade math test isn't going to make or break her chances at a successful future. It

Just-Been-There Advice:
Parents and Academic Pressure

Are parents' expectations unreasonable?

"A middle school girl I know says that if she gets a B, her mom takes everything away from her. I understand a D or F, but a B? Girls are already like, 'I have to get all As; otherwise I'm terrible or dumb.'"

—Nia, seventeen

There's a difference between a bad kid and a kid who doesn't understand math.

"I think parents need to understand when their kid is slacking off and when it's a real issue of not understanding the class. Instead of saying to girls, 'You're not doing well in this class and you're bad,' why not say, 'What aren't you understanding? Can you talk to your teacher?' Grounding her isn't going to teach her math. Instead, it could be: 'What can you do? What do I need to do to help you?'"

—Audrey, sixteen

It's drive, not grades, that counts.

"I know girls who think their mom will disown them if they get a bad grade. I don't think grades make you successful—I think your drive makes you successful. I think a B student who has drive will do better in life than a girl with all A's because her parents made her get them."

—Imani, sixteen

could be such a huge relief for girls if adults reminded them that they're loved no matter what—they're not *expected* to ace every subject. Since girls are so prone to create their own internal expectations for themselves, it can relieve the pressure to feel that the adults around them are cheerleaders, helping them cross the finish line—not just standing there with a stopwatch, clocking their time.

I've always been grateful that my parents didn't put a huge emphasis on grades and that they understood that I was capable of applying myself just fine. They both worked hard to send me to a private school, but they also supported all my extracurricular activities. Remember the anchor activity that I mentioned in the previous chapter, one of the three takeaways to downplay the drama? After realizing that playing sports had helped them in middle and high school, my parents saw the value in staying physically and mentally active outside school. They also wanted my siblings and me to be comfortable trying new things and understand the importance of commitment and following through, which are all essential lessons that we hope girls learn when they have an anchor activity.

You already know how important my dance classes were to me—mental escape, great exercise, and a way to de-stress and recharge. My sister painted and practiced gymnastics. My brother played soccer and basketball. It can be anything, as long as it's something your middle schooler loves to do and not something she's pressured to do solely because you want her to. Even though schoolwork is taking up more and more of their time during these years, girls who are involved with outside activities—especially ones that are physical and involve teamwork—say that they find them a welcome relief from stress. "Even though I feel busy at the activities, while I'm doing dance or field hockey I'll feel calmer," says twelve-year-old New York State native Taylor. To Taylor, the de-stressing impact of dance and field hockey outweighs the additional scheduling efforts and time consumed by these undertakings.

It might not be an obvious cause-and-effect situation—for example, your tween might not specifically say that her soccer practice is a great way to relieve stress—but if you've ever worked up a sweat on the field or at the gym, you know that exercising is a pretty surefire way to move that frustrated energy around the body and release endorphins, those feel-good chemicals. One of the greatest gifts my dance class gave me was the distraction from obsessing over other things: because my body was 100 percent engaged, I was unable to spend my time stressing over some perceived slight from a classmate. Hayley feels the same way when she's playing soccer, she says. Plus, the sense of inclusion that comes from being on a team allows her to take a step back and reevaluate her day-to-day drama:

> *"Playing sports calms me. I'm able to forget everything, all that drama, and just play. Usually after playing a game, after I've worked hard and gotten all that exercise, I sit and think about my life. Like, 'Okay, actually it is pretty good.' I think about all the good things that have happened. I think it's because I'm in a place that accepts me and I'm able to contribute, and I feel included. Even if we've lost, I feel like I've done something good."*
>
> —Hayley, twelve, Washington

Sports aren't the only way to relax, of course. Here are a few other outlets girls turn to:

Girls Talk:
What's Your Stress Relief?

- "Taking a long hot shower or watching a movie."
  —Kelly, thirteen, New Jersey
- "Playing with my cat and reading mysteries." —Emily,
  twelve, Georgia
- "Writing songs and practicing my guitar." —Bridget,
  thirteen, New Jersey
- "Read fantasy, historical fiction, and sci fi." —Taylor,
  twelve, New York
- "Playing the piano or flute. Lying down and listening to
  music." —Jessie, thirteen, Georgia
- "Sometimes I'll just sit and think. I'm not meditating,
  but I'm contemplating what's happened." —Kaitlin,
  thirteen, Georgia
- "I have all these inspirational quotes posted. I'll reflect
  on them and it'll help me—I'll think, 'I can do it, I can
  get this done.'" —Erin, thirteen, Georgia

Activities like these are necessary to girls. Whether it's
listening to their iPod or just reflecting on the day, these
girls all rely on their own methods of stress relief. To a parent, though, these girls might not look as if they're doing
much of anything. And you know what? That's okay.

I'm not saying that parents should promote unnecessary slacking off. But downtime helps girls process what's

going on in their lives and calms them down. Today's middle schoolers have far less free time than previous generations did, and taking back some of that downtime is vital, as twelve-year-old Sam can attest:

"Sometimes my mom thinks if I'm reading for a long time or listening to music that it's not very productive at all, but I still do it anyway. It recharges. I read and listen to music and pretty much do nothing, mostly after school or when I'm about to go to sleep. My mom pushes me to do different things—practice cello more, do more homework instead of having free time. I know I'll be able to get it done . . . maybe a few minutes after I'm supposed to get it done. But I really do need free time. If I don't have free time, I get annoyed with everyone. It calms me down if I'm angry about something, and it allows it to release, and gives me something to do other than schoolwork. And then I'm not angry at that person anymore."

—Sam, twelve, Washington

Aside from finding an outside activity and allowing more free time, our community of girls pointed to another important way adults can help them: teach them how to manage their time. "Sometimes I wish my parents would tell me to slow down," says Jessie, a thirteen-year-old in Georgia. "I have so much to do; I wish they'd just say 'Look, take it one step at a time, pick what you want to do most, and go with that. Don't let so many things pile up. Prioritize more and think more before you commit to something.'" They're looking to you to give them the permission to back off, not take on too much, and figure out how to prioritize what they *have* taken on.

Just-Been-There Advice: Love Your Planner

"In eighth grade, when I felt horrifically overwhelmed, I went to my guidance counselor and she talked to me about time management. We made an actual physical time line of when I would do things. I was able to prioritize my time for what's the most important rather than what I wanted to be doing. Now in college, I'm in two choruses, a sorority, and twelve different classes, but I still have time for myself."

—Grace, eighteen

Twelve-year-old Taylor says that having her mother's organizational help makes all the difference. "I have dance classes, rehearsal for two different shows, then field hockey every day after school for two hours," she says. "When my mom helps me lay it out, I know I'll get it done. I had a project last week, and I worried about when I could work on it in between practices. She helped me spread it out over a couple of days, and it was fine."

Some of the after-school activities that demand extra planning skills are vital. But some extracurriculars can be more of a stressor than not. How do you know if your daughter's new commitment to tennis will be the start of a new lifelong love—or something that will make you both miserable? High schoolers give you their advice on how you can recognize the difference:

Just-Been-There Advice:
Do What You Love

If she hates it, it's okay to quit.

"My mom's a pianist and all she wanted me to do was play piano. After seven years of struggling to practice, I finally told her it wasn't my thing. Once that pressure lifted, I could do something I really wanted to do—singing. It's really hard to tell your mom and dad that you don't want to play softball if that's what *they* want you to do. It was heartbreaking to my mom that I won't be a pianist. But once you let your kids do what they want, you feel like you're doing a good job as a parent because your kids are loving life and not dreading going to practices. In middle school, I chose my voice, and it made me happy and unwound me."

—Grace, eighteen

I gave up what was cool to find what I loved.

"At my middle school, the cool thing was to be athletic, and I didn't like that I was better at music. When you first met people, they asked, 'What sport do you play?' It was embarrassing to me that I didn't have one. I kept trying: soccer, swimming, cheerleading, dance, gymnastics, track. I was so bad; it's just not something that I'm naturally talented at. Dropping those was a big step toward antistressing. When I started to focus on piano, that positive motivation was a lot better than the negative motivation I was giving myself about sports."

—Haven, sixteen

There are less apparent ways to help your middle schooler too. Although my parents always listened to me talk about my problems with friend drama or other things happening at school, they sometimes didn't connect those problems to the way I was acting at home. Often I just wasn't myself. I'd feel pent up with stress after being harassed at school or eating another lunch in the bathroom, and it would reveal itself at inopportune times at home. Unintentionally I'd be short with my mom or lash out at my little brother and sister, causing my parents to yell, "Don't talk to your family that way!" Or I'd be sent to my room, where I'd cry and try to figure out how to pull myself together.

Looking back, I think what would've really helped was if my parents had asked me, "Is something going on? Can we talk through this?" These two girls say they'd like the same thing—to be taken seriously:

"When I tell my mom about something, I want her to help me, not make some dismissive comment. That makes me feel like there's no point in talking to her about it. I'd like to talk it out with her, for her to ask me questions, have a conversation, say, 'I'm sorry that's happening.' Just talking about it would help."

—Elena, thirteen, Washington

"When I talk about everything that's stressing me out, my parents act like I'm overexaggerating. I wish they would ask me what was actually bothering me."

—Erica, twelve, Georgia

Thankfully, I did have a few people to talk to, like Christie and the other older friends I'd made through dance.

That's why having a slightly older peer to confide in is one of the three takeaways. Being able to look up to someone and have that person tell you that you're not alone and that you *will* make it through can change everything. Here's some advice a few of our high schoolers received from their own mentors:

Just-Been-There Advice: How They Calmed Down

Fake it 'til they make it.

"My favorite teacher told me a way to reduce stress: reassure yourself. Even if you don't totally believe it yet, your brain and body are working together. So if I get a bad grade, I say, 'I can make it up; it's going to be all right.' Even if I don't feel it, I say it. And eventually my mind will be like, 'Yeah, we can do this!' Then you can use all that worry and change it to positive energy and work on the assignment."

—Kimmi, sixteen

Look to the past to predict the future.

"A mentor of mine said, 'If you want to figure out the future, look at the past.' I wish I'd known that during middle school. I'd done well academically and socially so far— so why would it be any different in the future? If I keep working as hard, the outcome will hopefully be the same."

—Britney, sixteen

I've found that both an older mentor and a parent can advise a tween girl in similar ways—but where the middle schooler might dismiss the parent, she'll listen to the older girl. (Remember that this is the time when a girl's primary influencers shift from her parents to her peers.) Even though my father tried to teach me time management skills, I didn't fully understand how important it was until Christie helped me find balance. She'd remind me that maybe talking to Mary-ashley or Lanier on the phone for an hour the night before a big project deadline might not be the best use of my time. I listened, and learned a lot from observing how she was able to complete everything she needed to accomplish, and do a good job of it too. My parents told me the same kinds of things, but it made a much bigger impact on me to hear it from a high schooler who truly understood what I was going through.

A big part of the stress I experienced was the pressure to keep up with the other girls in my class as they raced to have all the "right" name brands. I'll discuss that in depth in the next chapter.

Try This:
Help Her Counteract Stress

- **Try yoga or meditation.** Both are proven to dramatically decrease stress. Set aside time to take a beginner's yoga class in your area over the weekend, or download a yoga podcast and try it at home.

57

- **Get creative.** Unpack your arts and crafts supplies or sign up for a community pottery class together. Unleashing your inner artist is a great way to bond, de-stress, and channel your creative energy.
- **Crack up your stress.** Plan a biweekly or monthly comedy movie night. A good laugh goes a long way to alleviate the stress your tween is feeling.
- **Just for you: Walk the walk.** Are you constantly in overdrive and complaining about your stress level? It'll be hard to help your tween recognize and handle her own stress if she's getting the message from you that a sky-high stress level is necessary for success.

The Bottom Line

- Girls feel increasingly stressed out as a result of a host of pressures they're up against from external sources (parents, teachers, friends) to internal ones (their own expectations).

- The pressure to be "perfect" leads girls to feel terrified of failure and to strongly criticize themselves when they do make a mistake, however minor it might seem to you.

- Parents can help by recognizing their tween girl's stress for what it is: not waving it away or assuming that only adults experience stress.

- All three takeaways to downplay the drama will help relieve your girl's stress, but having an anchor activity can especially help channel her tense, keyed-up energy in a positive direction.

CHAPTER THREE

Who Has What

Name Brands, Materialism, and Competition

"I wish no one cared about this stuff. If you looked at me right now at home, no one from school would recognize me. I'm wearing baggy sweats, and my hair is in a bun. I wish I could just go to school and feel this comfortable."

—Rebecca, thirteen, Texas

When I left fifth grade for sixth, I wasn't just transitioning from elementary to a middle school; I was starting a whole new academic chapter. My parents sent me to a private school in our town with a higher percentage of wealthy families. I was worried about making a spectacular first impression on my soon-to-be friends and classmates. I wanted to look perfect.

A few days before school started, my mom took me to Old Navy to get a new outfit. After some careful consideration, pondering what each combination of clothes said about me, I settled on a dress, a collared shirt to layer underneath, and some cute shoes. I felt ready to face my unknown future: the new hallways, new classmates, and new teachers.

I remember that first day of sixth grade so clearly. As soon as I walked through the front doors of my new school and saw all the kids milling around, waiting for the bell to ring, I felt like I'd missed the memo: they were all wearing North Face fleeces over Gap thermal long-sleeved shirts and Timberland boots and were carrying L.L. Bean book bags. *All* of them. As I looked around at my classmates, facing the sea of North Face labels, I felt mortified—and horrifically out of place. I don't remember hearing any specifically mean comments from the other girls that day, but I was constantly on guard, certain that someone was going to make fun of my dress, which I'd loved hours before but now seemed hopelessly childish and lame. Halfway through the school day, feeling overwhelmed, I walked to the school office and asked to call my mom. "Am I not on the school mailing list?" I asked her. "Because I didn't know this was what you were supposed to wear."

After that first day, I immediately started to badger my parents. Obviously there was an unspoken uniform, and if I wanted to make it in my new school and be accepted by the cooler girls, I *had* to have those same Timberlands and backpack, the same thermals and North Face fleece. I *had* to. My social status and sense of belonging in my new school—that is, my life—depended on it.

My parents didn't really see it this way. They were sympathetic, sure, but with three kids and private school tuitions, they didn't have extra money to spend on random items of clothing that I felt I needed just because everyone else had them. We'd already done back-to-school shopping, and my mom was a creative, thrifty shopper. She looked great without caring about designer clothes and thought I could do the same. But she wasn't in middle school, where labels *count*.

One day early in sixth grade, I came home in tears. My red, blue, and yellow lunchbox, with my name inscribed on the front in puff paint, had suddenly become a target of ridicule in the cafeteria. "Have you not noticed that everyone uses a brown paper bag?" someone said during lunch. That snide remark was so cutting: it made me feel like a little kid, put in my place. "I will *never* use this lunch box again!" I vowed after school. (At the time, this felt like a matter of life and death.) And from then on, I asked my mom to use only brown paper bags so I could look like everyone else and avoid negative attention.

I had no idea why the cool girls in my class constantly made fun of me. But I thought my life would be a lot easier if I looked more like them, and a few simple shopping choices on my mother's part would make all the difference. Sure, it might mean that she was spending money our family didn't have, but wasn't my happiness worth it? Instead of the turkey sandwiches with Kraft singles, I needed to have peanut butter and marshmallow sandwiches—and only in Ziploc bags. ("Those are the cheap bags from Dollar Tree, aren't they?" one of the girls had pointed out over the cafeteria table.) I needed a Kool-Aid drink with a specific plastic top to accompany my new sandwich. Oh, and Mead Five-Star notebooks and mechanical pencils. I often sat in class wondering if I could get my mom to take me to Target after school and buy me these very particular things; I was so sure they would help me win approval—and, therefore, friends.

One day, after yet another specific and detailed demand,

Mom shot me a look and asked sarcastically: "Do you have any other rules? Because I've had it." I finally got it; it was exhausting for us both. (This was around the time that the verbal attacks I'd receive in the cafeteria compelled me to start eating in the school bathroom instead.)

Caring about the brand of plastic sandwich bags I used for packing my lunch sounds ridiculous now. But when I look back, I have such empathy for my seventh-grade self. I still feel the terror and hurt I went through at the hands of those girls, and I can see exactly what I was trying to do with those fixations, from the specific notebooks I requested (the Five Star three-ring binders in different colors) all the way up to the high-end clothes. I wasn't totally hoping that the popular girls would let me in their group; sure, that'd be ideal, but really, I just wanted some relief from the teasing. If I could fit in just a little more, I'd be a less obvious target, and maybe their mean girl spotlight would pass over me and land on some other unfortunate victim.

Little by little, I was able to acquire certain things that made me feel that I was fitting in. My parents wouldn't get me Timberland boots, so I spent Friday nights babysitting until I had the money to buy them myself. And by the late winter of seventh grade, I wasn't in the focus of people's mean comments; I blended in more, and the popular girls had moved on to targeting other people. And sometimes these girls would actually be nice to me—every so often they'd ask me to sit at their lunch table or invite me to a birthday party—which always felt so validating. Finally! They kind of liked me! The half-in, half-out thing kept me on guard, though, because I never knew where I really stood. But by the spring of seventh grade, I held out some hope that I might be included in their spring break plans.

Spring break and its accompanying bathing suits were a big deal at my school. A lot of the girls in my class had second homes on a lake forty-five minutes away from Albany, with their jet skis and family boats. A week at the lake was the prized spring break invite. Starting in January, these girls would buy multiple bikinis, which they'd bring to school in their backpacks to pull out for other girls to admire. I wanted to spend spring break at someone's lake house *so* badly that year, and I was hopeful that I would get invited. I begged my mom to take me to the store in our town that sold only swimsuits, where she balked at the $100 price tags. "This is ridiculous! Go look at the clearance rack," she told me.

I was determined to fit in: no half-priced swimsuits for me. Since my birthday didn't fall before spring break, my mom said I'd have to buy them myself. After roughly fifty hours of Friday and Saturday night babysitting, I was able to buy four bikinis at $100 each. I was filled with pride the winter day we drove to the store.

But I was never invited to the lake.

After all the hard work—first trying to avoid the popular girls, eventually vying for their friendship, saving for the right suits and buying them—nothing. No reward. I realized that this was never going to work. All of my attempts to fit in, this race for the best beach attire—none of it mattered because I was *never* going to be good enough for these girls.

I'm thankful that the summer turned out to be a life-changing experience for me. Letting go of the dream to be popular and leaving behind those social pressures meant that I could focus on other parts of my life— the things that I knew with certainty were positive and would help me grow. That's when I got really into the dance classes and where I met my new best friend, Lanier. And that's when I started volunteering at the Lions Literacy Center, where I met Amanda—a woman who didn't have enough money to buy basic cosmetics and household items. I felt ashamed by how fully I had accepted and perpetuated the rampant materialism at my school.

In the spring of my eighth-grade year, seemingly out of nowhere, one of those girls invited me to the lake. I went, and yeah, it was fun. But you know what? By then it felt like a pretty hollow reward.

The desire to have certain things has forever seemed important in middle school: the brand names may change, but the drive is always there. And that aspirational obsession with materialism, with having the "right" things, can follow us throughout our lives. Adults certainly try to valiantly one-up each other with their homes, cars, name-brand handbags, and other symbols of status. For girls, this begins in middle school, and it can either run its course, naturally letting up, or take hold and become intertwined with their self-image.

What makes it different now? The brands are getting more and more expensive and seem to be targeting girls at a younger age. For me, it was $60 Timberlands; for many of the girls I know in Atlanta today, it's $200 Tory Burch flats. I had really wanted $50 Gap jeans; girls I know today are spending $235 on True Religion jeans, asking for iPads for Christmas, and obsessing over Coach purses. They're reading *In Touch* and *Us Weekly*, watching fashionista teen dramas like *Gossip Girl,* and getting a healthy dose of materialism through celebrity culture and reality TV. They know what reality star Kim Kardashian buys, and they want that too. I'm not mourning the old days before reality TV and the Internet, but it's important to recognize this very rapid change.

Three girls speak to the ever-increasing price tag of popularity (Prada messenger bags!) and the social repercussions for not following these subtle rules:

"It's an unspoken pressure. If we're all sitting next to each other and I'm the only one not wearing jeans, Uggs, and a hoodie, I definitely feel it."

—Hayley, twelve, Washington

"People look you up and down during first period—they're seeing what everyone's wearing. You hope they're not going to make a bad face."

—Jessica, thirteen, New Jersey

"In fifth and sixth grade, you just threw things on and went out the door. But in seventh and eighth grade, it's like everyone's wearing Nike Air shorts. You just look around and suddenly realize that all the popular people are wearing Under Armour jackets, Juicy Couture, Coach, and Dooney & Burke, and if you don't, then you're not cool. You're a loser if you got your dress at Target. Not everyone can afford this stuff, but as I'm growing up, I realize that if you don't have a costly dress you're not cool enough or pretty. Everyone's carrying a Prada messenger bag, and if you don't have it you're a loser."

—Rebecca, thirteen, Texas

There's an underlying sense of unease in these stories. Objectively these girls see the label competition as a petty classroom game; as Grace points out on the next page, they know that it doesn't *really* matter whether a necklace is from Target or Tiffany's. And although they might genuinely want a North Face fleece, they also realize that the obsession with that particular logo is a sign that they're caving in to social pressure. But it's like a wave that they're powerless to stop: if they buy the right things and join in, maybe they won't get pulled under.

What's Behind the Materialism?

Every girl we interviewed, both the tweens and the teens, said that the switch to caring about name brands and "needing" certain things happened almost immediately on entering middle school. But why? Why does it become so important, and why is it so rarely discussed, like it's an unspoken undercurrent of middle school life? And why does it seem *so* essential during those three years?

From what I've seen with the girls I work with, I've come to feel that this materialism is a combination of insecurities and uncertainties that emerge at this time. It's not only driven by the social aspect of fitting in; it's also a form of comfort. Girls have gone from a safe, elementary school environment to being the youngest at a new school, surrounded by much older kids who seem to have a strong sense of identity and seem grown up. These younger girls are uncomfortable in their own skin, and even in the most supportive home environment, they can feel that they don't have an anchor. Interest in material things is one way for tweens to find solace while dealing with their new stressors. (Perhaps this is why it seems to affect the younger middle schoolers—those in sixth and seventh grade—the most.)

High Schoolers Look Back: We Dealt with It Too

"When I got to middle school, it was a sudden thing: I wanted a Coach purse. I didn't even realize why I wanted one. But it was because if I didn't have one, I wasn't a part of the in crowd."

—Brooke, fourteen

"In sixth and seventh grade, my mom never got me the Coach or Louis Vuitton bag; she was like, 'Why?' How do you explain to your mom that it's because you want to be popular? When girls say it out loud, it sounds silly, and they know it. And adults know it sounds silly too. They say, 'Don't worry about it; they'll like you for who you are.' But in your group, with your peers—you want it so badly, but you can't explain it to anybody else because it doesn't make any sense when you say it out loud. But in your mind, it makes sense: making friends is your top priority, and the only way you know how to do it is to find the things that attract them. And you wanted to feel like you were important enough to be able to buy something like that."

—Grace, eighteen

"Everyone had Hollister clothes and Dooney & Burke bags. I couldn't buy that stuff; we weren't rich, we were a Navy family. Also, I was a bigger girl, so the Hollister clothes wouldn't fit. I would try to, and that's where name-calling came in. It didn't look good on me. People would call me 'fat' or 'heifer.'"

—Kimmi, sixteen

It's a kind of transference. In the chaos of uncertainty about who they are and where they stand, girls can fixate on having certain things. Buying things—especially when they know that they'll help them feel included—can make everything seem okay.

That's how I see it, at least. But of course, to the girls who are living it (and to the high schoolers who have just gotten through the thick of it) the importance of what they wear is mostly about the opinions of their peers. Similar to how they often define their own self-esteem based on how others see them, the importance of name brands stems directly from their social circle.

Girls have no problem listing what types of clothes and accessories are must-haves in order to blend in, but talking about *why* they care so much means delving a bit deeper. Here, our tweens and teen girls dissect why that drive to blend in becomes a top priority immediately after walking through their middle school doors:

- **It's about finding her group of friends.**

  "It started in middle school because everyone interacted more. In elementary school, you made your group of friends based on your one class. But once you got into middle school, you could be friends with everyone. . . . It became, 'Oh, they're wearing a cute outfit today; I want to be their friend.'"

  —Courtney, twelve, New Jersey

  "I felt that if I dressed like my friends or looked like them, it would make us closer. Like, if we have completely different interests, maybe if I look like them, we can get along more. Because I felt like if I left the group I hung out with, I'd be alone."

—Elena, thirteen, Washington

- **It's about trying not to stand out.**

   "I'd always wanted to be part of the crowd. In middle school, when I saw people wearing Hollister and Abercrombie, I wanted to be a part of that. I'd go to Hollister and get name brand T-shirts just so people knew I shopped there. It's expensive, so I'd get the cheapest thing with `Hollister' written on the front so people can say, 'Oh, did you get that from Hollister?' 'Yeah, I was just in there the other day.'"

   —Kelly, thirteen, New Jersey

   "I care about having at least one of something. I want enough to fit in. I don't want to be that girl who's the wannabe who wants to have everything or the most; I care about having enough to get by."

   —Rebecca, thirteen, Texas

- **It's about getting along.**

   "It was a package deal: the kids who had the stuff hung out with the right people and seemed to have the most fun. If you physically fit in, it made it easier to get along with everyone."

   —Audrey, sixteen

- **It's about hope.**

   "You think that if you have the right things, that all of a sudden everything will change: that the one girl will notice you and say something about it, and you'd be best friends forever, and you'd be going to the mall and having sleepovers and doing things with the cool kids."

—Grace, eighteen

- **It's about finding herself, even when she doesn't know who that is.**

  "I think a lot of girls in middle school are trying to find out who they are or building up their own personality. People think that what you have defines you as a person. In high school, that's definitely changed; now people choose their friends more based on character."

  —Britney, sixteen

- **It's about impressing the older kids.**

  "If you look really good in eighth grade, the high schoolers notice you too, so it gives you a good high school reputation too."

  —Rebecca, thirteen, Texas

  "I sometimes think if I wore perfume and makeup, would the older groups accept me more? Would people see me as pretty?"

  —Hayley, twelve, Washington

- **It's about not falling behind the competition.**

  "Our grade is such a mental competition. Whether you're friends or not, you always look at what someone is wearing. I want people to say, 'What is she wearing?' I know a lot of girls who are known for good style, and I want to go to the same places as these girls."

  —Jessica, thirteen, New Jersey

- **It's about keeping her place in her group.**

  "Without me realizing it, my friends were pushing me to become more like the clique. I told my mom I wanted a Coach purse, and she got me a little clutch. I was so happy with it, even though it wasn't a full-on purse. You'd get an involuntary glare if you didn't have a Coach purse, so I always felt like I needed to have my purse with me. I was just trying to make everyone else happy and not get in trouble—I didn't want them to ask me, 'Where is your purse?' I didn't want them to exclude me."

  —Brooke, fourteen

- **It's about avoiding persecution.**

  "I always thought if I could have those clothes, I'd be loved by everyone: they'd see how good of a person I actually am; they'd treat me the same. I wouldn't have to worry about coming to school. I really liked school and love learning, but in middle school, I hated it because of the hallways. Since I looked goth, people would call me names and tell me I'm going to hell because of the way I dressed, or say, 'You're never going to amount to anything.'"

  —Kimmi, sixteen

As these stories show, there's so much behind the seemingly simple decision about what to wear to school on Monday. It's rarely just about throwing something on and heading to class. These sociological negotiations are happening all the time, as if every outfit choice determines a girl's place among her peers. And it's all happening somewhere in the back of your tween girl's mind. It's so subtle that girls might only think about it when they're asked directly.

Of course, these comments don't reflect every girl's experience. Often this materialistic obsession is more of an issue for those who strive to be popular, and not every girl cares about impressing the popular clique. "Usually those girls wear fancy stuff and talk about how it's expensive," says Kalli, an eleven-year-old Florida sixth grader. "For me, I prefer to have a low social status. When you're lower down, people don't pay attention to you, so there's less of a chance of people making fun of you."

To parents, it might not be apparent why this sudden increased interest in name brands can be damaging. For one, it can seem like old news: we all know that the social world falls into different strata based on what you own. You likely remember it from your own adolescence, and it might seem as if your daughter is dealing with an updated version of that. It could appear unimportant in comparison to the other issues we discuss—if your daughter isn't sleeping at night because she's stressed out, or if she's heartbroken because her best friend left, or if you're worried her calorie counting might lead to something problematic. After all, the obsession with name brands ends, right? And how can anyone stop it, anyway? Isn't this just the nature of middle school? What's the big deal?

It's not harmless, though. And in general, the shift into social groups based on who has what is rarely discussed. Parents often think, "Well, this is the way it is at this age," and either give in, hoping not to deprive their daughter, or they don't get what the big deal is and don't acknowledge that the pressure she's feeling is very real. But competition over who has the "right" clothes, shoes, bag, or phone—the message being, "Spend more money to impress us, and we'll let you in our exclusive circle"—is often hurtful and mean-spirited, and it can be a serious blow to girls' self-esteem.

"I feel small inside when they make fun of me for wearing clothes from Marshalls," says Bridget, a thirteen-year-old New Jersey eighth grader. No one should be made to feel small because of the kind of clothes she wears to school. When Veronica, a twelve-year-old Virginia native, is made fun of because of her clothes, she tries to remind herself that it's not about her; it's about them. "Sometimes people say 'Those colors don't go together' or 'I wouldn't wear that,'" she says. "It hurts my feelings, but it makes me feel like they're not true friends, and they're just saying that to feel better about themselves."

Here's why materialism is problematic, and why parents should pay close attention to whether their tween girl is falling victim to it, or even perpetuating it among her friends. For one thing, girls learn to place more value on (and judge others based on) material possessions and money rather than internal qualities. As the brands become more expensive, collecting designer items gives girls a false sense of entitlement, expecting that things should just come to them, without working for it. Hayley, a Washington State seventh grader, notes that not everyone can afford the same things: "I have one friend who makes me feel like we have to shop at Hollister. She'll say, 'Oh yeah, I was looking at the new bathing suits online. Were you? Did you order some?' And it's like, we don't have all that money to be looking at clothing all the time."

Also, when girls feel pressured to conform to the standards of others to fit in, they're less free to express themselves, explore their individual likes and dislikes, and find out who they are—the things they *should* be doing in middle school. "There've been plenty of times where I wear something and I'm really excited about it, and someone says something, and then I feel really discouraged and I won't want to wear it again," says Alex, age thirteen, in Washington. Bridget, a thirteen-year-old in New Jersey, noticed immediately that she was treated differently when she wore a popular brand to school: "I've never owned an Abercrombie shirt, but my friend left hers over at my house," she recalls. "On Monday I wore it, and I felt accepted. It was a good feeling, but at the end of the day, it didn't feel like me. The next day, when I wore one of my regular shirts, I went to go say, 'Hey, what's up,' to the popular people I'd talked to the day before; we'd gotten along then. Now they were like, 'Oh . . . hi,' and looked me up and down. It was a weird feeling. I was like, `Why would they do that?'"

And finally, competition among girls is amplified when they care so much about what they're wearing compared to the other girls. They're more likely to judge their peers, form social bonds based on exclusion, and waste emotional energy hurting each other. "It'd be better if no one cared—there'd be more complimenting instead of tearing each other down to the point where everyone goes home crying," says Rebecca, a Texan eighth grader. "If no one cared that you had the newest Betsey Johnson shoes or Nike Air shorts, it wouldn't be like that."

For Elena, getting dressed in the morning is a careful process, designed to help her not be judged in school. "When I get dressed in the morning I want to make sure I look okay," says the Washington thirteen-year-old. "I don't want everyone to look better than me. I compare myself to people, and not that I'm trying to beat anyone, but if one of my friends looks better than me, it makes me feel worse. This is all coming from inside myself—seeing what other girls look like and the pressure of trying to impress guys. I'm afraid one of my friends is going to say something mean and make it worse."

When girls talk about what's provoking their persistent demands for certain brand-name clothes, it's obvious that it's not just a harmless phase. As tweens can attest, materialism can lead to conformity, competition, and misplaced values.

So what about the girls who are making all the decisions and putting others down? What's going on with them? Eighteen-year-old Kendall reveals what was behind her own material obsessions:

High Schoolers Look Back: A Reformed "Mean Girl" Tells All

"If you didn't have the cool clothes, I didn't want to be friends with you. I'd be like, 'Why are you wearing that?' I remember turning thirteen and getting a Coach purse and matching wallet; I was like, '*I* have a Coach purse. Why don't *you* have a Coach purse?' At the time it made me feel cool to be in power. Looking back on it, it hurt a lot of girls.

At the time, I was thinking . . .
"I took comfort in the things I had. By showing them off, I hoped that other people would like me too because of it. I

really wanted to fit in, so I felt that if people saw that I had nice things, it would help me to fit in more.

In the end...

"I lost a few friends in middle school due to the bragging thing. One day, a girl gave me a note in between classes, telling me that she thought I was very stuck up and that I always flaunted the different things I had. She was like, 'People aren't going to like you because of the things you have; people are going to like you for you. I like you but we can't keep being friends if you look down on me because I don't have as much money as you or have the things you do.' At the time it really hurt me, but it was an eye opener that I needed to become more humble. I went home crying to my mom and showed her the note. She said, 'They weren't giving you this note to be mean, but to be helpful. Maybe you should take it as constructive criticism—something you need to change.'"

—Kendall, eighteen

Even if the tween girl in your life begs you for certain types of clothes (as I did with my mother) or to shop only at certain places, it's quite possible that there's a secret part of her that's conflicted about it. There's a part of her that knows that this cycle is relatively silly, as eighteen-year-old Grace pointed out at the beginning of this chapter. A part that's watching herself give in to the conformity and is frustrated by it —like Alex, who stopped wearing the outfits she liked. "I never thought I'd care about this stuff," thirteen-year-old Rebecca told us. "You hear yourself saying, 'I really need some new Nike Air shorts; everyone's wearing them.' I feel like I say that a lot now. And when I look like everyone else, I feel more accepted—but when I show everyone I have the shorts, it's like, 'Well, now what do I do?'"

So how can you speak to *that* part of her—that healthy skepticism? How can you help your middle school girl care less about material things and stay grounded and whole while dealing with these pressures?

You might feel powerless in the face of the demands for Uggs and Juicy jackets. Caroline, a middle school mom, feels that way:

"My younger daughter, who's only eight, now wants all of this stuff. It's who has the Mac, who has the newest Ugg boots. We all give in. This town is very competitive, lots of wealthy people, it's all about keeping up with the Joneses. They don't really understand that not everyone can afford this stuff. We're partly to blame because we indulge our children. We don't want them to be left out."

But parents are the ones who buy these items, after all—so the way you deal with your daughter's sudden new wish list can make a huge impact. I've seen parents who feel exhausted by the endless one-upmanship around brands, and I've seen those who buy into it because they're materialistic too. Of course you know this already, but still: the example you set as parents makes all the difference. If you accept and endorse it—either by buying all the Tiffany jewelry your daughter wants or by displaying your own obsessions with certain brands, shopping, and your appearance—you're not doing your child any favors.

As much as I would've preferred that my parents just buy me the Timberlands and L.L. Bean backpack, I'm *glad* they made me earn the money for the extra name-brand stuff I wanted. I realized that I was missing out on things with my friends because I was spending so much time trying to make enough money for a bikini. But what's even more important is that now, as an adult, I'm a pretty hard worker. That's something I learned in middle school that became a strong part of who I am; I internalized the message that you have to work for what you want. These high schoolers offer their thoughts on combating materialism.

Just-Been-There Advice: Girls Should Earn It

"In seventh grade, my parents started making me pay for a lot of the clothes. I babysat and learned to save my money. I quickly realized that I'd have to babysit three times for one shirt, so I'd find ways to get things on sale or buy things that weren't as expensive. It definitely made me realize that all of this was superficial."

—Dylan, sixteen

"If I wanted something, I had to earn it. So now, it doesn't feel right to me to get something that I haven't worked for; it hurts my conscience."

—Brooke, fourteen

Another tactic in addressing the problem of materialism is to circumvent the pressure. Here are some of the creative solutions developed by high school girls:

- **Get the minimum.**

    "You shouldn't go out and buy everything your daughter feels she should have. But if they *must* have one Aeropostale T-shirt to be happy, there's no harm in that. A lot of girls did that—we'd just get a few T-shirts and that's it."

    —Audrey, sixteen

- **Suggest that your tween lead the group with her own style.**

    "I've told my little sister that wearing the brands isn't important; fashion is about looking good. If she can create her own style, she can blow off the 'where did you get that, what brand is it' thing. Then it's like, 'Oh, wow, you have the cool clothes and look nice, and the brand doesn't matter.' I encouraged her not to buy things where brands were apparent, or to cut the tag out and just tell people it was itchy, or say, 'I don't remember where I got it.' Whatever you can say that lets it be about how the clothes or jewelry or purse is an expression of who you are. In middle school, it's about expressing that you're part of the group—but if you can *lead* the group, that's another thing."

    —Annie, eighteen

These are all great ideas, but there's one major thing that parents can do to really counteract materialism—one thing that I can guarantee will help your tween girl. It's one of the three takeaways to downplay the drama that I've found are consistently helpful to girls, across the board.

Volunteer a helping hand.

By "volunteer," I don't mean for one afternoon of one day a year (although if that's all you have time for, that's better than nothing!). I mean: Commit. Commit to an activity that has the potential to *mean* something to your daughter.

For me, that commitment was the real godsend. Working at the literacy center for years and helping Amanda gave me perspective that I never would have had otherwise.

There are many cool ways to bring service into these girls' lives:

- Make service a part of your daughter's allowance requirement.

- If you're a teacher, give extra credit for a certain number of community service hours.

- Make volunteering a requirement for taking a family vacation.

- Suggest she do her volunteering with a friend, her siblings, or the entire family.

- Sit down together and write out service goals for the year that you'll do as a parent-child team.

Even if you're driving your daughter to her first volunteering kicking and screaming, a service commitment is one of the best gifts you can give your tween girl:

- She'll see that, even at a young age, she really can make a difference and is needed in her community.

- She'll gain valuable life experience and perspective that will keep that materialism in check.

- She'll see what it's like to give back—to actively feel compassion for those less fortunate.

- She'll be grateful for what she has.

One of the sayings we use a lot in our Girl Talk meetings is, "Have an attitude of gratitude," and we try to emphasize the importance of feeling thankful. Not only does it keep girls grounded to realize that someone else had to work really hard to create opportunities for them, but taking the time to regularly appreciate what they have—from their house to their family to their health—makes a huge impact on their psychological and emotional health. Positive psychology studies have shown that feeling grateful is linked to feeling happier overall. And it actively counterbalances that sense of entitlement that we're seeing in younger and younger kids.

Plus, there's a great possibility that service will become a part of your daughter's life for a long time to come.

High Schoolers Look Back: One Girl's Wakeup Call

"Our group went to Goodwill together to volunteer. One of the girls who's well off was in charge of separating the clothes, and it was a really big reality check for her to be standing there and looking at the people coming in. Afterward she was just like, 'I don't even think about people having less than me, but they do. I was wearing $80 jeans and these people don't have $80 at all.' It's almost sad when you realize it's not important, because you feel like you've wasted all this time and energy on things that don't matter at all. In middle school, they're still young enough to be molded by that. It really makes a difference in their minds."

—Grace, eighteen

Just-Been-There Advice: It's Different in High School (It Doesn't Go Away, But It'll Never Be as Bad!)

"Every middle schooler is going to go through it; the degree to which it affects your life depends on how you handle it. People can let it go to their heads, or they can remember that they don't really need a watch to be cool. In middle school, it just seems that popularity is the most important thing, and often it seems to come from possessions. But in high school, I'm more confident and know myself more. I didn't need to have things to be liked."

—Colby, seventeen

"It's the same in high school—there are still certain brands, and you're in on it or not—but it's a smaller group now, and

I don't think it really changes your popularity. It's never going to be like middle school again, where it's like 'you have to have this to survive the social ladder.' You realize that if you can't get it, it's not going to be the end of your life. And your personality still matters, no matter what you look like."

—Audrey, sixteen

"By eighth grade, people started to realize that it wasn't cool to be just like everyone else. By then, you've fallen into what you're good at: band kids, football, chorus kids. You were in your own group and it wasn't about impressing everyone; you were okay with just being cool with your friends, and it mattered so much less. Nobody cared. But in sixth and seventh grade you think that everyone cares."

—Grace, eighteen

One cautionary note: Make sure your daughter is giving with the best intentions, without expecting anything in return or using her community service as an ego boost or a platform to self-promote or one-up her friends. She should be giving with a giving heart.

Committing to a service activity changed my life—and I've seen it change countless other girls I've worked with. It's the one thing that I can almost 100 percent guarantee will offer your tween girl some much-needed perspective. But even so, if nothing else, there's relief in knowing that this materialism is at its worst during middle school and that it really does lessen as she gets older.

Working with Amanda reminded me that it didn't matter whether I had mechanical pencils, or a certain kind of lunchbox, or four bathing suits. She used food stamps and had one pair of shoes; she teared up when I brought her some books from my childhood for her five-year-old son, because she certainly didn't have extra money to buy him books. Through my work at the literacy center I learned so much about the needs of others in my own community, and I saw that there were people whose problems were so much bigger than my own.

The greatest gift Amanda gave me was perspective: that what truly matters is our ability to relate to each other on a human level. That gift became an essential part of who I am today. Thanks to my work with her, I still carve out time today outside of Girl Talk to support causes I'm devoted to. It's why service is one of the key ways to downplay the drama: all of that emphasis we put on clothes and shoes and gadgets causes us so much unnecessary anxiety, when we could be channeling that energy into something positive.

You'll see these ideas in action again in the next chapter, where I'll tackle a close cousin to the materialism middle schoolers face: girls' insecurities about body image and the pressure to be pretty.

Try This: Help Her Counteract Materialism

- **Find the meaning.** Have your tween donate a portion of her monthly allowance to a charity that is meaningful to her. She can do the research to find the right organization, or you can seek one out together. Not only will she understand the importance of giving back, but she'll also find a cause that she believes in.

- **List important friend traits.** Sit down with your tween and make a list of what each of you looks for in a friend. Trade lists and talk about what's on each other's. Be sure that she lists internal traits, and not just external ones.
- **Volunteer on vacation.** During your next vacation, spend a day volunteering as a family with a local organization to show your tween that it's always important to offer a helping hand—even during a holiday.
- **Create piggy banks:** Together decorate a piggy bank with your favorite colors and designs. Choose a charity that you both believe in and use that piggy bank for your spare change. When it gets full, cash in your change and donate it to the charity. Keep filling it up as often as possible. Encourage your friends and family to give their spare change too.
- **Express gratitude.** What are all the reasons she has to be grateful? Discuss them with her and type them all as a list in her favorite font, then frame it in a picture frame you've picked out or decorated together. Or make a bead necklace together, with each bead representing one of the reasons she's grateful.
- **Just for you: Walk the walk.** Are you guilty of keeping this kind of middle school materialism alive? Are you actively searching out certain brands, or competing with your girlfriends for who has what, or promoting your daughter's materialistic interests? Remember that she's modeling her behavior on yours. It's vital that you show her how inconsequential materialistic goals are.

The Bottom Line

- While materialism usually increases during middle school, tweens are more affected by it than ever before, thanks to today's ultraexpensive name brands.

- Showing off name brands fills a number of tween girls' psychological needs, like fitting in, feeling safe, impressing the popular girls, and avoiding ridicule.

- It's not harmless or "just a phase": materialism harms girls' self-esteem and teaches them to focus on shallow surface values.

- Parents can help by realizing the importance of fitting in but not giving in to unreasonable demands.

- Committing to a volunteer activity is one major way that tween girls can gain valuable perspective and counteract the name-brand competition.

CHAPTER FOUR

Her Body, Herself

Body Image, Weight, and the Pressure to Be Pretty

"Being pretty is some girls' top priority. It's a very important part of being a girl. They think, `What's the point of being a girl if you're not beautiful and perfect?' To them, the ideal perfect girl is skinny and has long brown hair, and is super nice, and everyone likes her, and no one would ever mistreat her, and she's the coolest person in the world."

—Tabitha, eleven, New York

Early on during middle school, I'd sometimes be invited to sit with the popular girls during lunch. The conversation mostly revolved around the other kids in the cafeteria: who was wearing what, who said what to whom. A lot of times, they'd pick on other girls in our class and scrutinize their appearance: "Do you see her unibrow?" they'd say about a girl who hadn't started shaping her eyebrows. The *tiniest* things caught their attention, like who had wax in his ears or who didn't shave her legs.

This kind of intense criticism put me on edge. In sixth and seventh grade, my mom wouldn't let me pluck my eyebrows or shave; I worried that these girls were staring at my brows every day, and I never wore skirts or shorts for fear that I'd be called out for my hairy legs. Since I was often a target too, I felt constantly on guard when I sat with them: When would *my* appearance be up for discussion? I can't recall any specific moments when it was—but I absolutely felt that their judgment had a hold on me.

Middle school is the time when bodies change at varying speeds, and the discomfort that comes along with that easily manifests as teasing and scrutiny. Tweens feel an undercurrent of anxiety that they might be next in line to be picked apart by the girls or teased by the boys. "You're constantly worrying that someone is going to judge you for your looks," says Bridget, a thirteen-year-old in New Jersey. "As soon as you hit middle school, you start worrying about your weight. Eighth graders already know it, and when you're in sixth grade you're like, 'Wow, I have to look perfect to be in middle school or I won't get far.'"

In Chapter 1, I mentioned the perfect storm of changes that middle school girls experience: physical, hormonal, social, psychological, and emotional. Body image is often one of the main areas where these changes manifest. It makes sense that a newly found interest in appearance goes hand in hand with the name brand obsession. Suddenly your middle schooler is taking up precious bathroom time in the morning because her hair has to be just right; she's worrying that everyone is staring at her ears or her nose or her acne, or wondering if it's okay for her thighs to jiggle a bit when she walks.

She's experiencing growth spurts within a culture that

tells girls that being pretty is everything. She's expected to walk a line between looking cute for her parents, pretty to the other girls, and—a totally new thing—hot for the boys. And she's still trying to fit in, all the while hearing contradictory messages from the media, popular culture, and sometimes her family. And she's not even aware on a conscious level that she's engaged in this large-scale juggling act. What she does know is that her body is rapidly changing, and to differing degrees than her friends' bodies are—those she uses to gauge how "normal" she is. "Our bodies are so different than they were in sixth grade," says Alex, a Washington State eighth grader. "Now we're comparing—'Oh, my hips are bigger than yours.'" It's tiring just to think about it, isn't it?

Body image encompasses hair, makeup, skin, body size, and body type, but when most of us think of that term, we think about weight. And as our cultural fixation with weight increases (think of all the reality shows based around judging people, literally, on their weight), it's no wonder that younger and younger kids are developing eating disorders or are unhappy with how they look.

I remember girls in my middle school going to Weight Watchers with their mothers and counting out a certain number of Cheez-Its that they were "allowed" to eat. There were also girls who would walk around the track together in the mornings or afternoon, not because they wanted to be athletic and strong but because they wanted to lose weight. One girl only ate Saltines and drank warm water at lunch. To me, this certainly wasn't normal or okay. All of these girls seemed beautiful, and none of them looked overweight. I was so disturbed and saddened that their parents supported this kind of behavior. Girls today see the same thing:

"We had baked potatoes for dinner at Girl Scout camp, and one of the campers wouldn't eat them because she said they had too many carbs."

—Valerie, twelve, Michigan

"A girl I know is about the same weight as me, but before she eats anything, she freaks out: 'Do strawberries have fat in them? Am I going to get fat if I eat this?'"

—Max, thirteen, Florida

High Schoolers Look Back: We Dealt with It Too

"In sixth grade, I was the smallest girl in my class. My best friend was petite, but her boobs were bigger. You were conscious of that type of thing, because this is when girls are developing—and when you're not one of the five or six first girls, it seems like everyone is developing and you're not."

—Grace, eighteen

"I hated everything about the way I looked in middle school. I was chunky, my hair was an issue, all my other friends were stick thin and I wasn't. It definitely affected my day-to-day life. It was hard to not wear the clothes everyone else was wearing because I was bigger. I was self-conscious about everything and felt like I never looked good enough."

—Ashley, eighteen

Walking a Dangerous Line

"In class in seventh grade, we had to do a lab experiment where you used your body weight, and I had a guy friend who weighed the same as me. I took that like, I should weigh less; otherwise I won't be seen as pretty. I hadn't thought through that guys hadn't hit puberty and hadn't developed muscle. I started to become really worried about it. I would just eat my three meals a day and do all this sports practice and I started to lose weight, but my family was concerned because I took it to a new level. It had been, 'Oh, I'll make healthier choices,' and it turned into, 'I'm not going to eat any candy or snacks or french fries' until I started cutting out everything. For a few months I was in denial and didn't want to admit that it was unhealthy, because I liked being tiny. But to my family, my personality was changing because I was so worried about it."

—Alyssa, sixteen

Like the sudden importance of name brands, this new fascination with looks is partly about feeling included and fitting in: if you look like everyone else, you won't be excluded. But there are a few big differences about body image, like the fact that your body is changing—and rapidly. Alex noted that her friends already look so different than they did just two years ago; they're noticing and commenting on these changes, and often not in a gentle way. Growth spurts can be uncomfortable physically and emotionally, and often the way kids deflect their own unease is to put the spotlight on someone else. Tabitha, a sixth grader in New York, has recognized this too. "Girls feel bad about their own body image and they need to get their anger out," she says, "so they make fun of other people."

It might seem harmless, but that kind of ridicule can be devastating to a growing girl. In seventh grade, I had a friend named Sarah, an awesome girl with freckles, light brown hair, the best laugh, and the greatest smile. She was mercilessly taunted—her body had developed and the boys picked on her, saying she had an unflattering haircut. During a field trip that year, a boy she liked called her "Miss Piggy." I remember her crying the entire way back to the school, and she changed schools soon after. I hated that she felt that she had to leave school just to avoid the teasing.

Who Is She Trying to Impress?

"She's perfect. But she'll say, 'I'm fat.' I don't know how much is just talk and how much she really thinks that. She gets mad when I say she's fine. It's shocking to think that she can think that because she's a beautiful girl. All I can think is, 'No way! Why do you think that?'"

—Rachel, middle school mom

When girls tell me about their insecurities about their looks—how much they weigh, their hair style, their facial features—they say they have two groups of people they're trying to impress in the backs of their minds, and each one carries its own subconscious baggage: their **friends** and **boys**.

"I take how I feel about myself from my friends," thirteen-year-old Kaitlin says. Girls' thoughts about body image are similar to those about self-esteem: the image they see is intertwined with their perceived judgments from their friends and the people around them. These girls' comments show that their concern about others' opinions is paramount:

"Girls started talking about their weight right as sixth grade began, during that first month. If I went shopping with friends and I had to buy the medium and they were all wearing smalls, I'd feel really self-conscious. I just wanted to fit in. I wanted my body to be the same as everyone else— really skinny."

—Charlotte, twelve, California

"One of my friends has amazing fashion sense, so in the back of my mind, whenever I'm trying on clothes, I'm thinking, `Would Olivia like this? Would she think I look cute in this, or would I be cuter than her?'"

—Kaitlin, thirteen, Georgia

"It's important to me to be skinny, because you don't want to be the one who's self-conscious and not going to something. You'll be left out if you're not skinny."

—Jessica, thirteen, New Jersey

High Schoolers Look Back:
How My Friends Affected Me

"This is something we're doing now"
"In the middle of seventh grade—once the girls started to realize there were only a few attractive guys, and we were

all going after the same ones—people became more conscious of what they were eating. Everyone wanted to be thin and wear a two-piece bathing suit. During lunch, a lot of my friends would be looking at the calories on a pack of crackers, and it made me uncomfortable, but it was like, *Oh, that's something we're doing now.* So I started looking at calories, too. When I was with my parents, I'd eat whatever I'd want, but when I saw my friends eating really small portion sizes, I felt like I'd be the outcast if I wasn't doing that."

—Britney, sixteen

My best friend's issues rubbed off on me

"My best friend went through a period where she needed to have lighter hair, be thinner, shorter, and she started acting dumb on purpose. I knew it was a phase, and at first I let her go through it, but then I noticed I was reevaluating me too: Is how I look bad or different or not normal? I joined her in, 'Oh no! Do I need to change and dye my hair?' and saying I didn't know things, when I did. Finally I realized that wasn't what I was. We both came back to our senses."

—Brooke, fourteen

These girls are well aware that they don't live in a vacuum and that their own private opinions of their looks depends on how they assume their friends view them and what they think their friends will say. That's the subconscious baggage I mentioned earlier. When it comes to their girlfriends, they want to be seen as pretty and stylish. When it comes to impressing boys, that subconscious baggage is a little different.

Guys are the other big group that girls say they're sub-consciously trying to impress—and the reason your tween girl is taking *forever* to get ready for a short trip to the store. Somewhere around sixth grade, girls start to feel that they have new expectations to conform to. Attracting the attention of boys isn't so much about how stylish they are—that matters mostly among their girlfriends. Now it's about their "hotness," that ephemeral quality that's hard to define and is connected to their burgeoning sexuality and its accompanying complications and confusion.

Just-Been-There Advice: Don't Make Assumptions About What People Are Thinking

"I felt like a lot of times it was just me going through these struggles. I thought my friends were so pretty and flawless; I assumed they didn't struggle with any self-confidence problems or issues."

—Kendall, eighteen

"The truth is, everyone around you is just thinking about themselves. I'd catch myself thinking, 'What are people going to think of me?' But it doesn't matter nearly as much in high school. Everyone's just worried about themselves. It's like, I didn't even notice that your teeth are too big.'"

—Brooke, fourteen

But boys don't hit puberty as soon as girls do, and that disconnect makes this the prime time for boys to comment nastily about a girl's changing body. Whether they're an object of ridicule or desire, girls' bodies are suddenly topics of conversation among boys, and girls know it.

Girls say that they want guys to think they're attractive:

> *"If had longer legs or I was skinnier, I think my life would be better, because guys would like me more, which would mean I'd be more popular."*
>
> —Alex, thirteen, Washington

> *"In sixth grade you want to be pretty. In seventh grade, you want to be pretty and cute. By eighth grade, you either want to be cute, pretty, or hot."*
>
> —Max, thirteen, Florida

And they want to escape any teasing or harassment from boys:

> *"I'm really big-chested, and it's awkward. Over the summer I went to a carnival with a friend, and boys were following her around and harassing her because she had something written on her T-shirt. It made me really embarrassed. They were saying perverted things, and I don't want that directed toward me. I feel like I have to hide my shape because I'm worried about guys being gross."*
>
> —Valerie, twelve, Michigan

> *"We know our bodies are changing and we know we all look different, but guys in my grade judge you a lot just based off*

your looks. 'Did you see her in that bathing suit? She looks
so weird!' I was at the pool with a couple of my friends, and
one guy said to another guy, 'Look how hairy her back is.'
You hear guys making those comments, and it makes you
self-conscious."

—Alex, thirteen, Washington

Meeting all of these expectations can be confounding to girls, and the mixed messages coming from our culture make it worse. The media often flaunt displays of preteen sexuality under the guise that it's "cute"—we've all heard about thongs for elementary-aged girls, preschoolers who sing along to sexualized pop songs or mimic music videos, T-shirts for young girls with sexualized slogans—which confuses girls even more, since it's difficult to distinguish between what is age appropriate and what isn't. Is a thong "okay" or not? This all contributes to the pressure on girls to be "hot" at a younger age:

"For most of my life, girls haven't really cared about how
they look. Now they're more involved, because they're
excited about the fact that they're developing and getting
bras and going through puberty. It makes girls care more
about how sexy they look. One of my friends is obsessed
with being sexy."

—Tabitha, eleven, New York

In fact, many of the high schoolers quoted here, who are only a few years older than the tween girls, remarked on the obvious gap between their generation and their little sisters' when it comes to displays of preteen sexuality:

"It was shocking to watch these girls come out of fifth grade acting like ninth graders. In sixth grade, how much makeup does a girl really need? They were wearing eye shadow, foundation, mascara, getting manicures and pedicures every three weeks, and working out. They all had boyfriends. They sounded like thirty-two-year-olds."

—Grace, eighteen

"There's more pressure now to be hot. I go on Facebook, and you see these eighth-grade girls wearing such tight clothes and heels that they look trashy. I don't think they understand that guys will like them if they don't wear all that makeup. Facebook is an issue because you see older girls in photos and you think, `Well, they're wearing tight clothes,' but it looks more appropriate on them."

—Alyssa, sixteen

Just-Been-There Advice: You Still Need Personality

"If you're drop-dead gorgeous but have no personality, then guys aren't going to want to be with you. I try to stress being true to who you are and be a good person rather than someone who fakes, because then guys will realize that you're putting on a show."

—Britney, sixteen

When it comes to impressing guys, aside from the confusing mixed cultural messages, there's another new underlying social current to deal with: competition among girls. A girl who receives attention from a guy whom another girl wants or think she deserves can be perceived as a threat—and treated like one.

This was a problem for me in middle school. I didn't wear push-up bras and I hadn't even kissed a boy, but the older boys joked that I was "hot" and so I was on the "watch list." Though this was flattering, it was actually part of why I was so miserable at the time; that kind of attention made me even more of a target for the other girls. I didn't care what the guys thought; I just wanted the girls to like me, and I especially didn't want them to think I was playing into or trying to get this kind of attention. Plus, I was confused by it: there were lots of other girls who, in my opinion, were much prettier than me. What did "hot" mean, anyway? The whole thing made me feel icky, like I had a reputation for hooking up with boys, which was the furthest thing from the truth.

One day during eighth grade, I was walking across the parking lot to my mom's car in the carpool line when I noticed two other moms in line, chatting outside their cars while they waited for their daughters. These were the mothers of two girls who ignored and made fun of me, and when they saw me, they actually *glared* at me—looking me up and down and shaking their heads. It was obvious they were talking about me. What had I done to make even these adults hate me? I can only imagine what their daughters had told them about me—probably that I was hooking up with guys. I don't know if that's the case, but it certainly felt that way, since the girls' hostility toward me seemed to be connected to the fact that I was receiving unwanted attention from boys. I assumed they were spreading rumors, saying that I was someone I wasn't. The fact that even these *moms* were mean to me felt especially crushing. These were grownups I'd known my whole life. Was I missing something? Was I doing something wrong? I'd never even *kissed* a boy.

As soon as I got into my mom's car, I burst into tears. Thinking that I could escape the drama, we drove to the school Sarah had transferred to nearby to check it out. Sarah had told me over and over that I should go there, too, that her school was bigger and people weren't so interested in gossip.

I talked it over with my parents and my closest friend, Lanier, who'd also been experiencing this drama and came to the realization that I wasn't going to let anyone else affect me. My parents had worked hard to send me to a private college-prep school, and I knew it was in my best academic interests to stay. Even if girls spread rumors about me and shared them with their parents, they weren't true. Why should I change because of them?

So I stayed, and soon after, I gathered the courage to try out for the dance team, where I befriended Christie. Once she and her friends took me under their wing, everything changed: having an older girl, someone I looked up to, laugh with me and tell me she'd been teased too boosted my spirits like nothing else.

How It Holds Her Back

Even if your middle school girl isn't displaying obvious signs of body image problems—dieting, restricting her food,

High Schoolers Look Back: Slightly Older Mentors

"In seventh grade I was tall and skinny and played sports. Because I looked older than the other girls in my class, I hung out with some of the eighth graders. We shared the same clothes and had more in common. During lunch, I'd always sit with them, and they gave me advice. It helped a lot to have those older kids; they'd just been through what I was going through. My mom and dad would try to help, and I'd be like, 'You don't know what I'm talking about; you went through this so long ago'—it would go in one ear and out the other. But when I was talking to the girls who were closer to my age, I really listened."

—Imani, sixteen

obsessing about calories or weight—the added emphasis on looks can be harmful in more subtle ways. For one, feeling that she has to look like the crowd can lead to less freedom to explore how she *wants* to look. Fourteen-year-old Brooke says that after one of the girls in her Girl Talk group started straightening her naturally curly hair, she realized, "Wait, do I even *like* my hair when it's straight?"

If insecurities go unchecked, they can seriously hold these girls back. I've heard lots of stories from girls who actively chose not to do something—from attending a party to trying out for a team—because they felt so insecure about their appearance and didn't want to open themselves up to being teased—for instance:

"I love music and I wanted to try out for the chorus, but that same day I had a bad hair day, and everyone was making fun of me. So I didn't go to chorus tryouts. I didn't want to make the teasing worse."

—Bridget, thirteen, New Jersey

"In sixth grade I was self-conscious about my legs. I wanted to try out for soccer, but I didn't because I was self-conscious about the other people on the team compared to me. I just wiped that idea away from my mind. I know that doesn't matter as long as you're having fun, but at that time it did matter."

—Hayley, twelve, Washington

"Sometimes when I'm out with people I get so insecure—I should've worn these jeans or this shirt. I wish I could go home and change, or just not even be there. You're not really enjoying what you're doing because you're worried about the way you look."

—Alex, thirteen, Washington

What would've happened if Bridget liked her hair the day of chorus tryouts? Chorus could've been something that helped her soar and opened her up to a future full of singing; soccer could've been a great way for Hayley to relieve stress, get fit and strong, and work with a team. It's heartbreaking to think that these tiny insecurities about physical appearance held these girls back from fully discovering themselves and living their lives. Remember the

High Schoolers Look Back:
I Wish I Hadn't Let Fear Rule Me

"All throughout elementary school I thought, 'I'm going to play basketball when I get older.' I wanted to play so badly. But by the time I got to middle school, I didn't try out for the team because I was so self-conscious about my looks in front of the older girls. I was thinking, 'I can't do this because I don't look the part.' That's something I could've been good at if I'd tried. I definitely wish I'd done it. I had potential."

—Ashley, eighteen

dance story I related in Chapter 1, about overcoming my fear of being ridiculed to try out for the dance team—which ended up being a life-changing experience, since I met Christie. What would've happened if I'd let that fear rule me?

Middle school is the time for these girls to discover if they like playing softball, or debate team, or band. It says so much about the amount of pressure these girls are under that they'd allow their fear to keep them from trying something that they might fall in love with, something that might become a part of their identity.

Letting tiny physical insecurities get in the way of opportunities is one way that an emphasis on body image can hold girls back. There's another way, too—and it might actually look positive at first, since it can make girls feel closer to each other: bonding over self-criticism. I mean those "No, *I'm* so fat," conversations that these girls describe:

"It happens every day. Every day in the mirror it's like, 'I'm losing five pounds this week.' And it just goes on and on, and we'll sit there for five minutes looking at ourselves. 'Look at my nose! It goes so far! I need a nose job.' 'Oh my gosh, my legs jiggle every time I walk.' I think we analyze our body because we're going for compliments."

—Rebecca, thirteen, Texas

"'Look at all these jelly rolls!' Everyone is talking about how fat they are. It makes the girls feel like they have that in common—that they hate such and such about themselves—so they think that that's how you bond and become friends."

—Bridget, thirteen, New Jersey

"In sixth grade, girls started comparing their thighs. We'd be hanging out, and after we were done talking, we'd start comparing. It felt like, 'Oh, okay, every once in a while I have to be ready for this certain talk where we compare how we look.'"

—Hayley, twelve, Washington

"A few girls in my grade go to the bathroom in between every class period to make sure they look okay. It doesn't really faze me, unless they ask me personally: 'Do I look okay?' or they say, 'OMG I'm so ugly.' That bothers me, because they want people to say, 'No, you look really pretty.' I believe in positive reinforcement, but when you say that over and over and obsess, I feel like they're self-absorbed and all about themselves."

—Sara, twelve, Florida

Sara is on to something. This constant need for reinforcement definitely feels connected to a sense of self-absorption. As adults, we might not see that so clearly; after all, we can easily fall into these cycles too, and it probably feels more comforting than harmful. For your tween girl, it can be such a relief to know that she's not alone—that her BFF worries about her ears just the way your girl worries about her acne. But since they're still discovering who they are, these bathroom sessions can easily turn into self-loathing lists that only serve to reinforce obsessive interests in their looks, along with excessive comparison. There's a line between actual connection—gaining strength from hearing someone else's story—and reinforcing the already deep stereotypes about looks and femininity. Do you really want your tween girl listing her perceived physical faults in front of a mirror with her friends? There are much, much better ways to bond.

Try This: Healthier Ways to Talk about Her Looks

Grace, eighteen, successfully used these exercises with her Girl Talk group. They channel that desire to compare in a healthy way and draw out the positive aspects of sharing your fears without the harmful obsessing, nitpicking, and rewarding self-criticism:

"In my group, every six or seven meetings, we would sit in a circle and I'd draw out a name of one of the girls and read it out loud, like, 'Sarah.' The girl sitting next to Sarah would share one thing she loved about Sarah, and we'd go around the circle."

"We'd ask the girls to write down one thing they don't like about themselves. Undoubtedly, one of the other girls would say she loved the thing the girl hated. Like, one girl said she hated that she had red hair, and another said, 'I love the color of your hair! Brown is so boring.' Knowing that it was possible to love it, she wouldn't hate her hair so much. She'd have a whole new outlook. It takes only one person to say something that completely boosts your confidence."

What Makes It All Worse: Confusing Messages

At the same time that girls are dealing with body image pressures from their friends and guys, they're also dealing with a host of contradictory messages from the media. Girls know that the media hold up impossible standards of thinness and beauty. Many girls tell me they understand the magic of Photoshop, and they know magazine images are airbrushed and that women are made to look even skinnier on the page than they are in real life.

But that doesn't mean that the pressure doesn't affect them:

"I rarely see plus-sized models. On America's Next Top Model, they never have plus-sized winners; they always get kicked off."

—Kelly, thirteen, New Jersey

"In movies, they always make it seem like if you're not skinny, you're not good. The likable characters, the people you're rooting for, are always skinny."

—Kalli, eleven, Florida

"All the pictures in magazines are Photoshopped, but still—those are our idols. They're considered pretty, and we want to be pretty."

—Charlotte, twelve, California

These girls all know that they're looking at falsified images and impossible-to-achieve standards, but they still see that even with the caveat of Photoshop, models are pretty—and being pretty is still the ideal.

While the media are huge and inescapable influences, there's another one closer to home that has a huge impact on girls: their families. More specifically: Mom.

Of course, you know that your daughter takes her cues from you, but you might not realize how you're pushing your expectations onto her or revealing your own insecurities about your body. One grandmother I know obsesses over her granddaughter's weight and sends her photos of models in the mail. Girls have enough pressure as it is; they don't need more from their families—the people who are supposed to be their safety net.

My mom never once mentioned her weight, or hating parts of her body; she never counted calories or told me certain foods were off-limits. She just focused on staying active. She ran with a group several times a week, and my dad coached soccer; we all rode bikes together around our neighborhood. My parents imparted the message that it was more important to stay healthy and fit than to obsess over our weight or looks.

It's vital that parents don't reinforce stereotypes around weight and beauty. And not just through their own actions, but through their own media diets, and the media habits of your daughters too. Does that mean you turn off *America's Next Top Model*? No, but while you watch it, you might want to start an ongoing discussion about our culture's unrealistic beauty standards. This period is crucial for girls: it's when they create habits that will follow them for a lifetime. (Most girls who suffer from eating disorders develop them between the ages of twelve and fourteen, for instance.) You want to make sure you're setting a healthy example.

The moms of these girls have the best intentions, but

High Schoolers Decode: The Media and Growing Up Faster

"All of these TV shows where they're showing girls growing up faster: girls start to feel like they should be doing all of those things at a younger age. When people put so much emphasis on being pretty, it takes away from other things you could be doing at that age. You almost lose out on being a kid, you miss out on sleepovers with your best friends or doing things with your family, because you're so obsessed with looking pretty and meeting boys."

—Alyssa, sixteen

they're probably not aware of how their daughters internalize the messages they're receiving at home:

"My mom jokingly says I need to be skinnier and lay off the chocolate. It's not in a mean way, and I don't really get upset, but it does make me kind of want to be skinnier."

—Kalli, eleven, Florida

"My mom is one of the skinnier moms. She goes to the gym every day and it's a big influence on me. It's not a lot of pressure, but it's intimidating. If I'm like, 'Can I have pasta?' she'll be like 'Are you sure?' She'll ask me if I really want it. She'll say, 'But it's so bad for you.'"

—Jessica, thirteen, New Jersey

"I know my mom wants me to lose weight and I feel like she's rushing me into it. I know I should, but it's not really helpful to be told I need to lose weight. It's like, 'Okay, I realize that, thanks a lot.' I wish she'd give me more encouragement."

—Elena, thirteen, Washington

Elena also related a story about being out for dinner with some family friends. "One of them told me I was turning out to be really beautiful," she says. "It made me so happy. No one has ever told me that before. Hearing that from my mom would mean so much." Rather than "joking" about pasta or chocolate, maybe a gentler, more loving approach would work well, like letting your daughter know you think she's beautiful and then offering whatever constructive criticism you might have.

How Can You Help?

Maybe it seems like a lost cause—that it's inevitable that your daughter will leave middle school with a host of physical insecurities. But trust me: even with this perfect storm of pressures, influences, and confusing messages, it *is* possible to have a healthy body image during middle school.

In fact, many of the middle school girls in *The Drama Years* family say that of course they want to look good, but they're not obsessed with it. These girls show that it's totally possible for a tween girl to have a firm sense of self, with a strong body image:

> *"Out of all the things I have to think about, that's probably number 10 or 11 on my top 20 list. How I'm doing in school, how my friendships are, my relationship with my peers, my relationship with God, how well I do in sports: those kinds of things are all more important."*
>
> —Valerie, twelve, Michigan

> *"My mom asked me once: Would you rather be the smartest girl or the prettiest girl? I said I'd rather be the smartest because that will get me further than being beautiful. It's a good thing to be pretty, but it's never been my main priority. I've focused more on getting good grades so I can get a good job. But I've asked a couple of my friends the same question, and they've said they'd rather be the prettiest. I didn't understand: Where is that going to get you?"*
>
> —Tabitha, eleven, New York

One thing that girls with a healthy relationship to their bodies and their body image often share: they play sports. This makes sense. Exercise gives them healthy bones and muscles and releases positive-feeling endorphins, and it teaches them how to work with a team and how to collaborate with other girls instead of competing against them. But these girls are also seeing their bodies as something powerful—a way to make that basket or goal.

I've noticed that it makes a difference when parents promote athletics and activity and when they talk about being healthy instead of suggesting diets or exercise just to lose weight. Healthy means eating well and exercising—not to be skinny or conform to a certain body ideal—but to be strong, be fit, and stave off future health problems like diabetes and heart disease. Girls listen when their parents encourage this positive outlook:

> *"My mom doesn't talk about how she looks or say, 'Oh, I'm fat.' She works out a lot and isn't insecure about herself, so I think that's where I get it. I'm doing track, and I cheer. I'll go to the YMCA with my dad, and we'll do sprints for half an hour and lift weights, or bike around the neighborhood."*
>
> —Sara, twelve, Florida

Sara's active family is a great example of what can happen when parents mirror positive body image values to their kids. She sees that her mom is concerned about health, not weight, and she bonds with her father through exercise and activity. It's like they're all teammates together, supporting each other to stay physically fit.

Just-Been-There Advice: The Side Effects of Working Out with Your Family

"My mom used to be really overweight, and I was always a little bit overweight. We started walking around the park together every day one summer, and she stopped buying junk food and made healthier meals. She lost over 100 pounds from us all walking together. We'd have little discussions about what was going on in our lives, and it brought us closer together. It changed my relationship with my family, because every day I opened up to them a little bit more. By the end, I felt like I could talk to them about anything."

—Heidi, fourteen

Girls tell me that they like thinking of their parents as a kind of emotional teammate as well. "My family always compliments each other, like, 'I like your earrings' or `I like your hair,'" says eleven-year-old Tera. "I hear at least two every day. It makes me feel good about myself because it makes you feel like the day wasn't all bad." Rebecca loves the compliments she gets from her mom too:

"She'll say, 'You look so pretty!' 'Your skin looks good today.' She might say, 'Okay, you have a pimple,' but it's, 'Let's take care of it.' Or, 'We should work out or do something fun,' not like, 'Wow, you're big.'"

—Rebecca, thirteen, Texas

Since Rebecca receives so many kind words from her mother, when she gets a piece of constructive criticism—and it's said proactively—it doesn't hurt her feelings or come across as an insult. Likewise, twelve-year-old Hayley appreciates it when her mom points out something she thinks Hayley could improve. "If I tell her my stomach's bulging out more, she'll say, 'It's probably your posture. You need to work on it.' It feels supportive. I'm glad she points out that if I slouch, things will be worse."

Just-Been-There Advice:
How Our Families Dealt with Appearance

What Helped

"My mom complimented me on practicing, or it was, 'Congrats on your gold medal for dance.' It was about my achievements and accomplishments, not looks."

—Grace, eighteen

"I like that my mom would take me shopping and we'd get our hair and nails done. And Dad would tell us we're pretty every morning."

—Imani, sixteen

What Didn't Help

"My parents didn't boost me up or say, 'You look really nice today.' I didn't feel like I looked good enough for them. They'd talk about how big somebody was, and it'd make me feel bad about myself. It wasn't directed toward me, but I'd think, 'I'm not much smaller than they are, so what are they saying about me?' I didn't want them to say, `You're drop-dead gorgeous,' because then you know they're lying to make you feel better. I would've rather had them point out my good qualities."

—Ashley, eighteen

"My dad always called us his beautiful girls, but it actually upset me, like, 'You don't care that I don't think I look good.' I'd say I'm too skinny or I'm too tall, and there was no discussion of how it made me feel. It was just, 'You shouldn't be thinking that.'"

—Annie, eighteen

Of course, what most well-meaning parents *want* to say to their daughters suffering from body insecurities is something along these lines: *What you look like doesn't matter as much as how you treat others.* "If you can really let your personality shine through, then your body is just this vehicle for who you are," says eighteen-year-old Annie. "It doesn't define you." Your middle school daughter might find comfort in this truth, but it's much more likely to sink in if she hears it from—and sees it lived by—an older mentor. Hearing it from a high schooler, someone your child looks up to, will mean much more to her.

That's why a high school mentor—an adopted older sister—can be helpful during these discussions about body image. I've seen it over and over again within Girl Talk, and I clearly remember it from my relationship with Christie: it's much easier to talk to a slightly older girl about these anxieties and pressures. Mentors can reassure girls that these concerns are totally normal, and they can boost a girl's self-image and self-confidence to a dazzling degree: they can tell her why they think she's beautiful. She'll be much more likely to believe compliments if they're coming from a supercool older girl she admires and isn't part of her family (in other words, someone who doesn't "have to" think she's gorgeous, the way parents might).

Plus, if there *is* a reason for alarm—if your tween is obsessing about weight or appearance—an adopted older sister is the perfect person to bridge the gap between adult and child. She can tell you about any red flags that might come up in her relationship with your tween, while still respecting your middle schooler's privacy.

The other two takeaways to downplay the drama are also vital here too. Through a service commitment (lending a helping hand), girls learn to appreciate what they have, and it takes the focus off the obsessive scrutinizing of each other's looks. I know that for me, volunteering at the literacy center was a wakeup call: clients there often didn't have access to dental care and couldn't afford the bare minimum in terms of clothes—and *I* was obsessing about a potential unibrow? It can be incredibly powerful to remind girls that while they're worried about their acne or being too tall or too short, lots of people in their community are trying to find a place to sleep at night.

I've talked about the importance of sports throughout this chapter, but if your tween's anchor activity—the third takeaway to downplay the drama—is show choir or community theater or an orchestra or a political organization, she'll still reap the benefits when it comes to body image.

Just being able to channel her energy toward something other than her insecurities or the drama at school can be a godsend; it will allow her to focus on something she genuinely cares about instead of fixating on her body. And chances are that that anchor activity, whatever it is, will introduce her to a community of like-minded others who care about the same thing, people who will appreciate her strengths and accept her for who she is and what she has to offer.

We'll talk about the power of accepting people for who they are—and what happens when girls *aren't* accepted—in the next chapter, when we discuss what it means to be a good friend.

Try This: Help Her Keep a Healthy Body Image

- **Make a reality-versus-fantasy collage.** Create two collages: one with images of people she respects, like friends, family, relatives, sports stars, and public figures. In the other collage, feature pictures of celebrities, models, and movie stars. In a glance, she'll be able to see the difference between the people who really inspire her and the false images the media feed us.
- **Let her plan healthy meals.** Once every two weeks or so, let her take over the kitchen and make something healthy and tasty for the family. Together, look up recipes and pick out ingredients at the grocery store.
- **Get active.** Make one Saturday or Sunday a month a

designated family activity day: go hiking, swimming, or bike riding together.

- **Create affirmation stickers.** Using adhesive labels and sharpies, have her list the physical attributes she loves about herself: her eyelashes, her strong muscles, the way she can run, the cool freckles on her arms. These affirmation stickers can go on her locker, notebook, or on a small mirror that she carries with her in her bag.
- **Just for you: Walk the walk.** Are you mirroring unhealthy values around body image? Does your middle schooler hear you complain about your body or your looks? Remember that she's internalizing these things and that your behavior will be a model for her.

The Bottom Line

- Girls experience a perfect storm of physical and emotional changes during middle school that often lead to a period of increased self-consciousness and insecurity. Their feelings about themselves come from how they think others perceive them.

- Girl's burgeoning interests in guys, and mixed messages from the media about what level of "hotness" is appropriate at this age, can leave them confused and add to increased competition for boys' attention.

- Negative comments from parents about looks, hearing their own parents talk badly about themselves, or hearing that losing weight is more important than staying healthy exacerbate the confusion about body image.

- Physical activity is an important counterbalance to mixed body image messages. Incorporating the three takeaways—an anchor activity, a helping hand, and an adopted older sister—can take your tween's mind off obsessing over her looks and help her focus on more positive values and goals in her life.

CHAPTER FIVE

BFFs, Frenemies, and Mean Girls

What It Means to Be a Friend

"Sometimes I just want to go back to elementary school where everyone was friends and the biggest thing we fought over was sharing crayons."

—Courtney, twelve, New Jersey

By now you know that I dealt with a lot of mean girl situations throughout middle school. I've told you how I spent sixth and seventh grades trying to fit in with the popular girls, to no avail. Sometimes they'd invite me into their inner circle, but mostly I'd just hear about parties I hadn't been invited to or weekend plans that hadn't included me. Those were only the passive ways that the girls at my school made me miserable; sometimes they could be seriously aggressive.

There's one instance that I'll never forget. One time during seventh grade, I was at home on the computer while my parents were out running errands. I signed on to AOL Instant Messenger, and saw that my friend Neil, who was a year ahead of me and felt like an older brother I could confide in, was on too. "How's it going?" he asked. "You looked sad in the hallway yesterday."

"I've had a rough week," I typed. "I just feel like no one likes me here. I don't know if I want to come back here next year."

I had hoped he would say something like, "Aw, don't let them get you down, you know you're awesome," like he normally did. But instead, he wrote back: "Well, Haley, you *are* really snobby."

What? I was shocked by his response. *Stay calm,* I told myself. *He must be telling you the truth for your own good.* "Really?" I wrote back.

"Yeah, people think you're fake," he responded. Suddenly, he sent a flurry of IMs: "You think you're too good for everyone." *Send.* "You should probably go to a different school." *Send.* "In general, you're just an annoying bitch." *Send.*

Each time a message popped up on my screen, I felt my stomach lurch. Tears sprang to my eyes. *This* is what everyone thinks of me?! I couldn't take it: "Thanks for telling me, Neil," I typed, and then signed off. I was in shock.

Actually, Neil hadn't written any of this. I later found out that he'd been swimming in his pool—not sitting at his computer—the whole time. So who was pretending to be him? Three of the popular girls who taunted me almost every day—the very same girls I was confiding to him about. They happened to be at Neil's house and decided to bait me anonymously.

It was totally devastating, and from talking to girls around the country, I know that this kind of cyberbullying occurs all the time. (If your tween girl gets through middle or high school without going through something like this, consider yourself very lucky.) By now, we all know that girls can be mean. They're not always nice and sweet, and they can quickly turn on each other, backstab, and bully.

When it was happening to me years ago, this was pretty major news. Although everyone knew it often occurred among middle schoolers and teenagers (either because they'd seen it, been a victim of it, or perpetuated it), it wasn't really openly discussed until movies like Tina Fey's *Mean Girls* and books like Rachel Simmons's *Odd Girl Out* and Rosalind Wiseman's *Queen Bees and Wannabes* appeared. Now we hear about bullying and mean girls everywhere—on TV and in movies, in pop songs and in news headlines.

We've heard the devastating cyberbullying stories. We've heard about Phoebe Prince, the fifteen-year-old whose suicide led to the enforcement of stricter antibullying laws in her home state of Massachusetts, and Megan Meier, the thirteen-year-old who killed herself after the mother of a classmate bullied her on MySpace. As the bullying epidemic in the United States grows, the media attention on those extreme stories is an important public service, and we're seeing new antibullying organizations all the time doing great work to counteract this major problem, groups like It Gets Better, Rachel's Challenge, and the Kind Campaign, all dedicated to preventing bullying in schools or offering solace to those who've been bullied.

I'm relieved that the problem is now a major topic in the news, and I cover "mean girls" and bullying in this chapter. But since Girl Talk is all about being proactive and positive, I didn't want girl-on-girl aggression to get all of the attention here. So instead, let's look at the basic day-to-day interactions of friends and the very real heartbreak and pain that girls experience as their social groups change and friendships break apart. Often what gets lost in all the gawking over the drama is what it means to actually have—and be—a good friend. After all, once she's left the confines of her family and before she's head over heels in love, no one else holds a middle school girl's heart and mind like her friends.

Maryashley was my best friend until she moved to Las Vegas during the spring of my sixth-grade year. That's why I didn't really care about the other girls before middle school; I had Maryashley. We hung out all the time, wore the same kinds of clothes, and participated in the same activities. But once she left and when Sarah transferred, I felt completely alone. That's when I started to want the other girls to include me—those girls who eventually tricked me over Instant Messenger. It felt like they were constantly changing their opinion of me. As much as I wanted to be in their circle, it might've been easier just to be excluded altogether, because then I would've stopped trying. It was the back and forth that drove me crazy.

At the time, I thought I was the only person going through that kind of torture. Today I see girls who are dealing with it every day. Without a doubt, friends (and all the complications, disappointment, and gifts that they bring) is our number one topic at Girl Talk. Most middle school girls count their friendships as a top priority—so when they shift and change, fall apart and reassemble, it can feel as if the world has turned upside down. Dealing with the roller-coaster ride of friendship can be one of the hardest things they'll go through. These girls recount some of their painful friendship moments:

"At the beginning of sixth grade, I had a group of friends who were kind of mean to me. At lunch, they told me the

guy I liked asked me out. I knew it was a lie, but they went on saying, 'He wants to go out with you; go talk to him.' They wanted me to go over to his table just to humiliate myself. I said, 'Look, if you don't tell me the truth, I'm going to move to another table'—and the threat of me moving to another table was too great to bear, so they told me. I felt really hurt and betrayed, and I wondered why they'd want to do that to me. I'd never been mean to any of them; I'd only been a good friend."

—Valerie, twelve, Michigan

"My friend Bonnie decided she didn't want to be my friend anymore. Now all my friends are hanging out with her. I don't know why she's mad at me, but she ignores me when I say her name. I have other friends, but now my best friends aren't talking to me—so it's like, 'Do I stay with my best friends forever, or should I find new friends because they're being mean to me?'"

—Rebecca, thirteen, Texas

These are the kinds of stories that make parents throw up their hands and say to their girls, "Why can't you *just be nice* to each other?"

Why is friendship so incredibly tough in middle school? How can two girls who've been best friends their entire lives suddenly turn into enemies? It seems that out of nowhere, a girl's best friend becomes a frenemy—a sometimes-friend, sometimes-enemy—and she doesn't know whom to trust. A friendship takes years to build, and at this age, one small action can bring it tumbling down.

I remember feeling just as fickle about my friendships sometimes. I'd be ecstatically looking forward to having a friend stay over on Friday night, and then I'd overhear her say something mean to someone else, causing me to feel completely over her and no longer want her to come over. Best friendships become fair game, easy to throw away. Robert, a middle school dad in California, says he's worried about what lessons that might teach his daughter. "Her biggest issue is loyalty among people she thinks are her friends, that they might leave her for someone else," he says. "My biggest fear is that she'll learn from these experiences that people aren't willing to work and put the effort into a friendship that could last a lifetime. She'll think that friendships and people are disposable."

When girls tell me why they think friend problems are so earth-shatteringly hurtful in middle school, a few key points stand out. For one, these girls are dealing with a great deal of change all at once, and, in general, life feels much less stable in middle school than it did before. So that means that these breakups and fights can hurt that much more because they're rocking already shaky ground. Thirteen-year-old Jessie in Georgia explains it this way: "The drama is pretty prominent in your thoughts, because it's like, if that doesn't work out, who's to say your other friendships will work out? That something won't happen between your parents, say? Who's to say that everything won't crash because one thing crashed?"

One of the major changes they're all going through is puberty. Since they're growing up at different rates, they're naturally going to have less in common with some friends and more in common with others. (These are the years when it's not uncommon for tweens who still look as if they're in elementary school to be sitting next to girls who've already gotten their period and are wearing bras.) And as their bodies change and hormones fluctuate, so will some of their interests and priorities. Girls who used to do everything together can suddenly see each other very differently. A lifelong best friend can seem hopelessly young—still playing with kid stuff—or much older and more mature, to an intimidating degree. That's what happened to Taylor, a seventh grader in New York:

"My best friend since childhood dropped me in sixth grade; it was awful. She started hanging out with a whole new group, and I didn't know any of them. She and her friends would call boys. I went over for a sleepover once, and they were calling boys and asking them to rate them on a scale of 1 to 10. I felt really uncomfortable, so I just sat there, and it was a very awkward feeling. She's much more superficial, materialistic, more into gossip. I was sad because we'd been friends for years. Sometimes I'll see old pictures of us, and it'll be disappointing."

I encounter this over and over among the girls I work with. Watching a friend change into someone they don't know leaves them feeling abandoned, left out, and scared that perhaps the same thing will happen in their other friendships. It can be a shock to see someone they've known their whole life—someone they depend on to help them feel stable—go through a transition. To thirteen-year-old Elena in Washington, it was devastating to realize her friend was changing:

"When I met Amy, she wore mixed-matched clothes and she read all the time. I sat across from her our first day of fourth grade, and we just clicked. But in sixth grade,

*her attitude started to change toward me. She became this
not very nice person, kind of snotty and so different. She'd
gone from floral prints to black sparkly T-shirts. And then
I started to not trust her as much because we were getting
so distant. Like, okay, I'm not going to tell her tons of things
that she might tell other people because we're not as close
as we were before. It became hard to be friends with her.
She began to not tell me things, and I was the last person to
know; it was like, this is weird, what did I do? I started to
think it was my fault. Other friends have changed, but our
friendship is the same—I still see parts of them that I know
from before. With Amy I feel like she's almost trying to be
better and impress people."*

Changing is a natural part of growing up, of course,
and many girls do recognize that. "In sixth grade, I had a
group of four best friends, and now we don't even hang out
anymore," says Charlotte, a twelve-year-old in California.
"We all spread off into different groups. It's sad. We had
sleepovers and were so close and told secrets all the time.
I guess we're just finding out who we are, and we found
somewhere else where we thought we belonged."

Being perceived as the one who has changed can be just
as painful as being left behind. I try to remind girls that
transformation is what middle school is all about: these are
the years that you're supposed to experiment with your
interests, your style, what you believe in. This is where parents can step in and remind their tween that not all growth
is bad, since she's still figuring out who she is, and while
her old friends might not understand yet, they'll also go
through their own changes.

A girl's social group will often morph as quickly as

her body and interests do. Many times, girls are forced to choose between their old friends and new ones—and in the process, some can be left behind. Jessica and Valerie experienced this firsthand:

"In sixth grade this very exclusive group formed, and one of my best friends went in it, and I didn't. They had a name and basically didn't really talk to anyone else. They're all nice alone, but when they're together, they didn't talk to anyone else. It hurt my feelings, and it just broke our friendship. Now people want to be in that exclusive group, but they still want to be with us, and we can't let people be with us or them: you have to choose one. Do you want to be with the people you can trust or people who'll turn on you? It hurts my feelings to see my best friend two days ago talking to my old best friend from two years ago, because I'm worried she's going to leave us and join that group."

—Jessica, thirteen, New Jersey

"All of a sudden Mandy dropped me like a rock and went for this mean girl, Erin. They were obsessive BFFs and completely ignored me. Finally, one day I said, 'Mandy!' She said, 'Don't call me that. Call me Amanda.' It's like, where did my friend go, what happened? I said, 'You have to choose: me or Erin,' and she said, 'I'm sorry, but it's Erin.' Realizing that one of my best friends dropped me for another girl who called us mean names for years was too much. It was really painful."

—Valerie, twelve, Michigan

Just-Been-There Advice: We Dealt with It Too

"I had no idea that my friends were talking about me behind my back, saying, 'She's ugly' and 'She's so weird.' I was heartbroken when I found out. An acquaintance told me they were talking about me, and at first I didn't believe her. I was like, 'Oh, that'd never happen.' But then I walked into the bathroom one day, and the girls were standing there talking about me: 'Why does she always go to tutorial in the afternoon?' 'I don't know how to get away from her; she's so clingy.' I was shocked. I didn't say anything; I just turned around and walked out, and I was like, Okay, I'm done. For the rest of the day, I felt stunned. I was thinking, 'Wait, are they right? Am I really clingy? Do I really not have any friends?' I started questioning myself. I felt like I'd been betrayed. I couldn't let go of that feeling; I saw them every day, so I was constantly reminded. I started hanging out with another group."

—Britney, sixteen

"A friend of mine got mad at me for standing up for myself, and she stopped being friends with me. That's when I knew that she wasn't a real friend and I couldn't trust her. It was the first moment I ever remember doubting or questioning my friends. I'd always been so trusting, and the realization that not everyone is going to be completely trustworthy was weird. That's when I started to realize that everyone wasn't nice. It took a big toll on me. I feel like it changed me as a person. I started to see there was bad in the world."

—Haven, sixteen

High Schoolers Look Back: I Ditched My Friends

"If a more popular girl wanted to have me over, sure, I ditched my friends in a second. And pretty soon I was part of that crowd. But my new friends weren't as academically focused as I wanted to be, so near the end of eighth grade, I had to make a decision: Am I going to hang out with these people or study? When you turn down an invitation three weekends in a row, they're going to stop inviting you, so I drifted away and back to my other friends. I'm sure they were hurt, but they welcomed me back with open arms. I missed good times with them in middle school because I wanted to be part of a better group. And even when I was hanging out with the popular group, I liked being smart and actually reading the books and doing my homework. So when I went back I was, like, I can be that person now without worrying about that or being laughed at."

—Annie, eighteen

What's All the Drama About?

"My friends have this need for drama. It's like the oxygen that blows through their lungs. They can't live without it."
—Tabitha, eleven, New York

Not only is all that change actually dramatic for girls, but the word *drama* is a favorite catchall term. Their school is

131

"drama," their friends are "drama," this or that situation caused "so much drama." But why do girls create drama—instigate fights, spread rumors, turn on their best friends, and ice people out—for no apparent reason?

I don't think girls mean to do these things. From what I've seen at Girl Talk, it's usually unintentional. (And girls often think it's everyone *else* creating the drama, while they're innocent!) It's a combination of insecurity, jealousy and roller-coaster hormones that can easily spin out of control. Most of the time it's only a few girls causing 95 percent of the drama. The challenge is to learn how to throw water, not fuel, on that fire.

According to the middle and high schoolers interviewed for this book, the impulse girls have to create drama stems from several sources:

- **Wanting a feeling of power.**
  "Some people feel like if you turn against someone, it means that you're cool," says twelve-year-old Courtney, a seventh grader in New Jersey. "It's like they're throwing away part of their lives to be on top for a year."

- **A fear of confrontation; not knowing how to honestly and safely express anger.**
  Alex, a thirteen-year-old in Washington, describes it this way: "If you have a little problem with someone, you're quick to turn on them because then you have an excuse to be mad at them. Something's happened in the past that you haven't forgiven or you're not okay with, so you're quick to pounce on them because you're still insecure about something else."

- **Taking something superpersonally.**
  High schooler Britney, sixteen, explains: "Girls can
  do things without thinking that end up hurting their
  friends. Often it seemed like the girls who start the
  drama are so fixated on getting the attention that they
  don't realize how badly they can hurt someone."

This probably sounds similar to the drama you might've
experienced among friends when you were in middle
school. But there's one huge shift among this generation of
girls: the reliance on technology to tear each other down.
(Just like that IM session of mine years ago.)

As much as we all love our smart phones and chat sessions, our digital communication makes it incredibly easy
to bully someone, instigate or heat up fights, or just mistake
someone's joking IM for an insult. "It's really easy to start
a fight over text, and to just say something mean because
you don't have to see the person right in front of you," says
twelve-year-old Charlotte, from California.

A 2011 poll from MTV and Associated Press found that 50
percent of teens have experienced "digital abuse": harassment over text or Facebook, forwarding of private photos
over e-mail, and so forth. Now that so much social interac-
tion is happening over these media, instead of in person or
over the landline, it's even harder for a parent to keep track
of her middle schooler's social interactions. Taylor and Alex
describe how they've seen technology exacerbate fights
among girls they know:

"Girls get into the most vicious fights over Facebook. Curs-
ing each other out, saying, 'I hate you,' just losing it. One

girl drops a comment as her status like, 'I'm so mad about such and such,' and the other girl says, 'Don't you say that about me,' and it gets into a huge argument. Then people make jokes about it; guys say, 'Rowwr, catfight!' It makes it less private because tons of people know that you're getting into a fight."

—Taylor, twelve, New York

"There's been lots of cyberbullying at my school. Someone will know someone else's Facebook password and will go onto their account and say how slutty they are. It's like, Don't trust anyone with stuff like that! In a way it's scary, but it happens so often in the community I'm in, that pretty much all you have to post is, 'I love when people hack my account,' and then it dies down. But everyone still thinks, 'Well, it is true*, or 'That* would *be something you'd say.'"*

—Alex, twelve, Washington

Technology is changing lightning fast, and so are these interactions. In fact, even our high schoolers are surprised by the changes they've seen.

High Schoolers Decode:
How Tech Changed Everything

"Technology is causing more problems than it's helping. People are sending out big group e-mails and not including other people. We didn't have that in middle school. Cell phones were just coming in and we weren't texting; we were just calling our parents."

—Alyssa, sixteen

"Most of the drama takes place on the Internet. Technology is causing a lot of drama that wouldn't have even existed before. When I was in middle school, if you didn't get invited to a party, you might not even know that everyone got invited. Now you'll know because everyone's on Facebook saying, 'I'm at a party with these people,' and you weren't invited."

—Audrey, sixteen

All of this drama is undoubtedly hurtful to your tween girl. It's heartbreakingly painful, and it can put a huge dent in her self-esteem as she wonders what's wrong with her or what she did to make her friends act a certain way. For many girls, these breakups are their first experiences of deep interpersonal trauma. Who can they trust? Who won't throw them overboard? It might be the first time that they realize that things can go wrong, that people might not be what they seem. It's a tough lesson, and it's unfortunate that girls have to learn to be careful whom they trust.

"I'm careful with what I say to my friends. If your friends turn their back on you, then they know your secrets. I tell my friends lame secrets like, 'I have a crush on that person,' but I don't tell them what actually happens with my family drama. I don't know who I can really trust, and that's why

I don't tell anyone anything anymore. At any second that friend can just turn on you, and they'll know everything."

—Charlotte, twelve, California

"People say they're your friend and tell you all this stuff to your face; you think you have this bond, and they totally shatter it when you find out they've talked to the guy you liked and they've told him things you've said about him. Who can I trust? Are they going to change over the summer? Over next weekend? You thought they were your other half, part of your world, you're the U.S. and they're Canada, you go together like peanut butter and jelly. Then you find out that the peanut butter has salmonella."

—Jessie, thirteen, Georgia

"For every four or five friends you go through, there's one who's really trustworthy and special. You have to spend a lot of time with them and see if they talk badly about other people or act differently around you versus another person."

—Hayley, twelve, Washington

Just-Been-There Advice: Girls Shouldn't Jump into Being BFFs

"Don't call everyone your friend until you know you can trust them. Don't think just because you've known them for a month or two that you're superclose."

—Nia, seventeen

"You just want somebody you know is going to be there when you're upset and have exciting news to share. It's hard to find someone like that. I always tell girls: `Don't just pick some random girl you think will be awesome and throw all your secrets on her. You have to test people out before you know that they'll be a good friend.'"

—Ashley, eighteen

Not knowing who they can confide in and constantly keeping their guard up: these are distressing things to hear about our tweens, to know that at twelve years old, they've already decided they can't really trust each other.

Wondering who they can trust is an internal consequence of all the girl drama; there's an external consequence too—the fact that it's a major distraction in school. "It'll totally consume my mind," says thirteen-year-old Jessie from Georgia. "I can't think about anything else. While your mind is running through this friendship issue, you completely withdraw and autopilot through your homework."

The exact same thing happened to me. I got all A's, every semester, until the spring of my sixth-grade year, when I received my first C. I was filled with anxiety in the classroom, worrying if the note I saw being passed was about me or if the girls were laughing at my outfit. Sometimes it felt like I was on the verge of a panic attack.

Who *can* concentrate under such intense circumstances?

"If it gets really bad, I can't think of anything else and I'll start crying and there's no way I can do my homework. I

can't focus. It takes away from school a lot, because you don't think about the friends you do have or the good things in life; you're only thinking about that one problem, and it takes up your whole life."

—Kelly, thirteen, New Jersey

"In class, I didn't have a problem focusing, but once I got home and people started texting me, then I couldn't focus on my homework, and that really lowered my grades. Either I didn't finish my homework, or I stayed up 'til 10 working on it because I was wasting so much time texting them, trying to figure everything out."

—Kaitlin, thirteen, Georgia

Watching your daughter experience friend drama—to see her iced out from interactions with so-called friends, bullied, or left behind—is incredibly painful as a parent. It's hard not to advise her to retaliate somehow, thinking that at least it's better than watching her feel sorry for herself.

But these are perfect opportunities to set her up to have stronger female friendships for the rest of her life. As we know all too well, some of this frenemy and mean girl behavior doesn't end in middle school, and it's up to parents to help their girl recognize right and wrong behavior. These are the years where she can really learn what it means to have a good friend and what it means to be one herself.

My mom did a lot to teach me these lessons firsthand. You'll remember that middle school was pretty lonely for me. After Maryashley moved to Las Vegas and Sarah transferred, I felt unsure of my social group. Where were my best friends?

Around the same time that Sarah transferred, we were working on tumbling in my PE class. I was a good dancer but terrible at gymnastics—I couldn't even do a cartwheel. To pass the class, we had to do tumbling moves in front of everyone. I had crazy anxiety leading up to it since I knew I wasn't good, and that it would just give the girls more fodder with which to persecute me.

In the locker room on the day of my failed tumbling attempt, I could hear the other girls making fun of me while I changed inside a stall: "Can you believe she doesn't know how to do that?" "She can't even dive." "She can't do a cartwheel. That's why she quit gymnastics." I thought some of these girls were my friends, and I wished just one of them had stood up for me and said, "Hey, she's really sensitive about this."

I started to cry as I vented to my mom after school: "I hate this school! I hate all of this! I miss Maryashley and Sarah. Am I ever going to have real friends?"

"I'm sorry this happened to you, but it's not the last time you'll be under a spotlight, doing things you're not comfortable doing," my mom said. Then she did something that totally took me out of my problems. "You know, Sarah's been having a hard time," she reminded me. It was true: Sarah had just changed schools, and her old friends weren't including her in any sleepovers or parties anymore, plus she was dealing with a lot of family trouble at home. "What does she like?" Mom asked. "Let's bring her a surprise."

I immediately perked up—I could rattle off twenty things Sarah loved! Plain M&Ms, blue raspberry Mr. Misty, LipSmackers lip gloss, TCBY'S white chocolate mousse. My mom was basically saying: *Okay, you had a bad day, but look at what Sarah's going through. Focus on being a good friend to her rather than on why these girls aren't good friends to you.*

While Sarah and I ate frozen yogurt and did our homework together, I told her about tumbling. Later I realized how wise it was for my mom to suggest doing something kind for someone else to take the attention off me. With my mom's help, I took a situation that could've made me bitter, and instead, it made me better.

To this day, I try to use this bitter-versus-better concept when I feel hurt by someone. Okay, so someone said something mean; I can choose to let that situation make me bitter, hardened, mistrustful, or I can figure out what there is to learn and move on.

Maybe this sounds Pollyannaish. But I don't think there's anything naive about the power of kindness; it should be a core value for each of us. You never know what someone else is going through, and you can absolutely make someone else's day by just choosing to be nice and kind instead of thinking solely about yourself.

These are the lessons that the tweens I work with at Girl Talk seem to crave. I've found that three values in particular do wonders for girls, particularly around friendship issues:

- **Kindness**
- **Authenticity**
- **Humility**

Kindness

I think my mom was on to something when she emphasized being kind to Sarah. There's a kindness comeback these days. Ellen DeGeneres's signoff on *Ellen* is, "Be kind, everybody," and lots of schools have adopted kindness measures to counteract the rise of bullying. More and more positive psychology studies have shown how cultivating kindness makes us happier in general.

Here's one way that we try to actively and immediately bring in kindness in our meetings and camps: we ask our girls to stop before they speak and reevaluate what they're going to say based on this acronym:

True

Honest

Important

Necessary

Kind

Is what they're about to say True? Is it Honest? Is it Important? Necessary? Kind?

We ask them to T.H.I.N.K. before they speak, text, or type and try to incorporate it into their daily lives—especially within their interactions with their friends and classmates—as much as possible. It's a choice girls can make: Do they want to encourage others with their words, or bring others down?

You might think this won't resonate with your middle school girl, but I promise that it works. It's not about self-editing or asking her not to speak her truth, of course; it's about thinking of others too.

Authenticity

You've probably heard your tween disparage someone else for being "fake." While this often seems like a blanket statement, a reliable stand-in to describe some kind of behavior that doesn't represent her sense of who the other girl is—there is something to be said for sticking to your guns. As your middle schooler searches for who she is, it can only be helpful to emphasize that she work on her own authenticity rather than falling back on calling others "fake."

Humility

Today's tween girls probably don't remember a time before Paris Hilton, the socialite who's famous for no particular accomplishment. It's no wonder that more and more girls have said in polls that they want to be "famous" when they grow up—not a doctor, or a lawyer, or an astronaut. In their book *The Narcissism Epidemic,* psychologists Dr. Jean M. Twenge and Dr. Keith Campbell posited that today's teens and tweens are growing up with an alarming sense of entitlement about their place in the world and their futures. Studies have shown that social media promote narcissism by rewarding us for obsessing over our daily lives in a whole new way.

Whether you believe that narcissism is an epidemic among today's young people or not, there's certainly a lack of humility these days, and it's another quality that can only make your middle schooler a better friend to others and attract similarly true friends.

I realize we're living in a time where meanness rules, a

world of snarky blog posts and angry anonymous commenters, where we revel in others' failure on reality TV shows and are accustomed to increasingly hostile political campaigns. It's a world where these values I've mentioned might seem archaic and obsolete. But at Girl Talk, we're

Girls Talk: How Do You Know You Have a True Friend?

"My friends now make me feel really special and good, like, wow, no one's really cared about a friendship this much before. Just little things made me realize this. Like when they asked me what I was going to wear to the dance, and I mentioned this one pair of shoes I had— and they knew, even though we hadn't bought them together or talked about them; I just wore them sometimes. It surprised me that they were that involved. They'd be on vacation and call me if they knew I was home. It's obvious they care about my feelings and my life."

—Taylor, twelve, New York

"My best friend and I make each other laugh so much and we're true to each other. We tell each other all of our secrets, and we trust each other so much. We spend so much time together and have so many connections. We disagree, but that makes it interesting."

—Tabitha, eleven, New York

on a mission to bring kindness, authenticity, and humility back—even make them cool—because they work. Cultivating these values will not only make your middle schooler happier; she'll also attract better, truer friends. Frenemies fall by the wayside, because they'll see she won't waver and she's going to stand up for what's right.

Girls crave this kind of stability in their own lives and in those around them, and they need affirmation from the adults in their lives that these values are truly important to their future happiness and success in relationships.

Try This: What Is She Looking For in a Friend?

If your middle school girl is having friendship troubles—fights, friends turning on each other, seemingly unnecessary drama—here's a conversation to have: What is she looking for? What kinds of characteristics does she want in a friend? What's her ideal friend or friendship? Then ask her if she thinks she has these characteristics. Even if she says yes, ask what she could work on. What would make her a better friend?

This exercise is similar to my mom's suggestion to me about how to cheer up Sarah, as it helps her think about how she can be a better friend rather than focusing on how she's been wronged in the past. And in general, it's good for a girl to know that sometimes she will have casual friends who don't want the best for her, or who talk badly about her, and she doesn't have to write them off; she just shouldn't spend too much time thinking about them. She should focus on the *good* friends she has instead, the ones who encourage her and lift up her spirits.

"My mom suggested I pray for better friends who were loyal and trustworthy and honest and weren't going to manipulate me. Every morning I'd pray for friends, and eventually I did end up with a lot of friends. For girls who aren't religious, maybe they could think about what they look for in a friend. Even if the person they get along with the most isn't popular, it doesn't matter."

—Valerie, twelve, Michigan

My parents taught me another valuable lesson about friendship: Don't be quick to throw them away. It's like dinner plates that you wash versus paper plates that you throw away. We're so quick to think of our friends as paper plates—something that can be tossed away at any point. (And this is even more true now as communication becomes increasingly more disconnected and not in-person.) But if parents support this mind-set, they're setting girls up for a lifetime of bad behavior.

In my family, it was superclear that no matter what, we were expected to work out our differences—and my parents wanted that to extend to my close friendships too. I remember when a friend hadn't invited me to a sleepover and my feelings were hurt; I cried all weekend, knowing everyone else had been over at her house, having fun without me. "You need to work this out," my mom said. "You've been friends for too long to not ask her what's going on." My mom actually drove me over to her house, where I found out that my friend was secretly mad at me because the guy she liked had asked me out even though I didn't like him. If I hadn't approached her about this, it could've turned into a friend-turned-enemy cold war at school, where I retaliated by not inviting her to *my* upcoming birthday party, and so on. My mom happened to be particularly in tune with how to navigate my friendship dramas, but here's what our tweens said they wanted the most from *their* parents:

- **Just be there to listen, not to tell them what to do**
  "You don't always need advice; you just want someone to listen to you or hear you out or hear your side."

  —Kelly, thirteen, New Jersey

  "Advice frustrates me. I don't want advice, I just want to talk about it."

  —Valerie, twelve, Michigan

- **Distract them**
  "Help me get my mind off it by doing fun things."

  —Kaitlin, thirteen, Georgia

  "My dad's very calm, and he gets my mind off my problems. We talk about stuff greater than me and my petty problems, like politics."

  —Valerie, twelve, Michigan

- **Give them two free "drama" days**
  "Two days a year I'm allowed to call my parents and they'll pick me up, no questions asked. Parents might

think it's silly to leave school, but they don't know how hard it is."

—Charlotte, twelve, California

• **Remind them to think about the other person**
"My mom will say, 'Do you notice she does this a lot? Maybe that's something you need to work around.' Or she'll take me to the other side of things, how they're feeling, and it's like, *Oh, that makes sense why they're acting that way, then.* And she'll suggest I confront them in a nice way: 'Hey, I heard you told Angie this, but that's not really what happened. Why did you do that?' That helps a situation so much more than getting really angry."

—Alex, thirteen, Washington

And here's what both middle schoolers and high schoolers said *didn't* work:

• **If it's not an emergency, adults shouldn't call the school . . .**
"I get really nervous if my parents try to take it to the school. Then those kids will hate you, and everything gets worse. An adult going to the school creates more drama."

—Emily, twelve, Georgia

• **. . . or the other girl's parents.**
"I'd say, 'They're leaving me out. What should I do?' And my mom would say, 'Do you want me to call their parents?' I was like, 'NO!!! I just need advice.'"

—Heidi, fourteen

Just-Been-There Advice: You Never Know Who Might Be Your New BFF

"You should always extend yourself to people you think you might not get along with—because you might. If you get excluded from your group, take a chance and talk to someone new. You can get along with a lot of different people. It's good to always have someone else to turn to."

—Audrey, sixteen

- **Don't suggest other friends.**

  "My mom understood how big my friend drama was, but the things she'd say would frustrate me and make me not want to talk to her: 'You shouldn't have cliques; you should hang out with this person.' I'd say, 'You don't understand, I'm not friends with that person. I can't just go hang out with her. That's awkward and weird.' And she'd say, 'Well you can *become* friends with her!'"

  —Fiona, sixteen

Of course, one of the biggest things that helped me deal with friend drama in middle school is one of our three take-aways: an adopted older sister.

Christie helped me navigate friend issues. When I hung out with her, I felt accepted, included, and wanted. And she *totally* understood what I was going through. As awe-

Just-Been-There Advice:
Get Specific

"My mom didn't allow me to use curse words, and I think that helped a lot. I couldn't say, 'She's such a bitch.' If I had a problem with a girl, I had to say, 'She did this and that made me angry because . . . ' If I'm not using words like that at home, I'm not really using them around girls, and it made it easier. If you say, 'She's so rude,' and it gets on gossip train, it's better than, 'She's such a bitch,' which is like gossip wildfire. Plus, using adjectives helps break down the core of the problem rather than the overlay of one word that combines everything. 'Bitch' is the one thing where people are like, 'Oh. I get it, I understand.' But if you say, 'She always talks to me in this voice and that upsets me because . . . ,' then you're really talking about the issue."

—Grace, eighteen

some as my mom was, talking with her just wasn't the same as talking with Christie.

I had been lucky to connect with Christie through my dance team, but not everyone has a built-in mentor to turn to. That's one of the major purposes of Girl Talk: to connect high school mentors with middle school girls. It's an immediate partnership. You don't have to just wait and hope that your daughter meets a fantastic, trustworthy high school girl, though. You can be the catalyst. Is there a babysitter you trust? A girl down the street? A daughter of a close friend? A cousin? If there's a high school girl in your community whose values you admire, reach out and ask her to take your middle schooler under her wing.

This has happened to me countless times over the years. Parents have said, "Hey, can you take my daughter to breakfast on Saturday?" Or, "My daughter has had a rough week. Can you pick her up after school and take her for ice cream?" If you think your daughter would benefit from the help of an older girl, you can make it happen.

High Schoolers Look Back: How Our Mentors Helped Us

"I went to my neighbor a lot more than I went to my mom. I'd go over after school and do my homework at her house, or we'd sit outside and talk. I felt like my mom wouldn't exactly give the best advice. My neighbor is a lot of fun, and it's really easy to talk to her; plus, I didn't want to start crying in front of my mom, because she'd just look at me and be like, 'It's okay, sweetie,' but not really know what to say. My neighbor had a lot of really good advice and seemed willing to listen. She really put it in perspective and made me think back on the situation and think out different scenarios."

—Britney, sixteen

"I have a neighbor who's two years older than me. Her influence was really helpful. She's really down to earth, and if I was ever fighting with a friend, she'd give me good advice—she'd stay calm and not be so dramatic. I was grateful to have advice from her, not just a parent or teacher."

—Brooke, fourteen

"My mentor was a big sister to me. I knew she'd do her best to be there for me. It definitely changed things for me, because she could pull out some awesome advice. I'd come to her with something that was so negative and she'd change it around to be more positive. There was a girl who was being supermean to me and I wanted to be mean back or start a rumor. My friend said I needed to kill her with kindness, not to let her know it was getting to me. It totally worked, even though it was hard to be the bigger person; I had to constantly remind myself to do it. But I was so thankful I'd done that."

—Ashley, eighteen

Over and over, our middle schoolers have said that while they haven't shut their parents out of their lives, they absolutely don't confide in them as much as they used to because their parents just don't get it. But a slightly older girl will. (It doesn't even necessarily need to be someone who's a few years older; it could be someone who's a grade just above or an especially relatable adult.) Every girl we interviewed who has had a mentor in her life says that she benefited greatly from that relationship:

"I feel like I can hold it all in, but I want someone to know about it at the same time, so they can help me. I tell one of

my dad's friends about my drama. She doesn't tell anyone;
she's kind of like my friend at school, but she's an adult.
She's like a free therapist."

—Charlotte, twelve, California

Our other takeaways to downplay the drama are vitally important here too. As I mentioned in the previous chapter, when your tween finds an activity that she can channel her energy into outside school, there's a good chance she'll also create a new social group, which can be incredibly important when friend issues arise at school.

After Maryashley left for Las Vegas and Sarah transferred, I relied on my new friendship with Lanier at my dance studio even more. Since we didn't go to the same school and she wasn't involved in the details of the classroom drama, we could lean on each other during our time dancing or when we'd sleep over at each other's house. My friendship with Lanier felt safe, and I wasn't worried that it would falter or fade away.

Besides offering much-needed perspective, a volunteer commitment—the second takeaway to downplay the drama—can be a powerful way to bring girls together. Girls who've been fighting or keeping a cold war going in the classroom often bridge that gap through connecting during a service activity. Their petty differences can pale in comparison to the actual suffering they might see while lending a helping hand together.

As you might imagine from all of my stories about the mean girl drama, finding and recognizing my true friends has been a journey for me. It didn't happen as soon as I started high school, or when I launched Girl Talk: it wasn't until college that I realized who I should be devoting my energy to—and who I shouldn't.

When I started my freshman year, I went from a super-hectic high school schedule (academics and Girl Talk and dance and babysitting!) to a very open one, and suddenly I had a lot of free time on my hands. I had also broken up with the guy I'd dated throughout high school; I just knew we both needed to move on. Several of our mutual couple friends didn't feel the same way, and a lot of people I'd considered close girlfriends instantly distanced themselves from me, because in their minds, I'd hurt my ex-boyfriend. We used to all go out as couples together, and once the two of us broke up, my girlfriends didn't feel comfortable meeting me for dinner or a movie because they felt that they'd be taking my side. The guys all stuck together like glue, but my friendships with those girls faded away. It was painful, and I thought the only reason they were my friends to begin with was out of obligation. Meanwhile, I was desperately missing Girl Talk— I'd left behind the one thing that I was truly passionate about.

That first college Christmas break was a turning point for me. I came home unsure of who my friends were, since it seemed that I'd lost many of them in the breakup. But I also came home to an outpouring of letters from middle schoolers and teenagers. Girl Talk had received its first big publicity with an article in *CosmoGIRL!* magazine, and girls from all over the country were asking how they could start their own chapters. For me, it was a wakeup call: I had to get back to Girl Talk, and I had to let go of trying to win back my high school friends who didn't even seem to care about me.

I made a list of all the people I knew I could count on: my family, Lanier, Maryashley, Ms. Presley, Mrs. Lentz, and others. Then I made a list of all the people who often seemed to be happy when I was unhappy—people who drained my energy. It was very clear: one list was a group of people I started to think of as my "sunshine team," and the other list was a group of energy "vampires." Right then and there, I made a conscious decision to channel my support into my sunshine team instead of wasting my time with the energy vampires.

It was pretty amazing how quickly my life turned around once I made this change. Focusing on my sunshine team seemed to attract more positive energy in my life in general. Once I stopped trying to placate all those people who drained me, I had more time to be a better friend to my true encouragers. And through their support, I found the drive to keep going with Girl Talk and try to expand it beyond my one high school.

This could be helpful for your tween too: to think of true friends as her sunshine team and to let her know that it's better to have two amazing encouragers in her life—people who will cheer her on—than to have eight energy vampires who are always tearing her down or pointing out the negative things.

Try This: Help Her Counteract Friend Drama

- **List the pros and cons.** When she's going through a hard time with a friend, have her list the positive things she gets out of the friendship. Then ask her to list the ways that friend might hurt her. Comparing the two lists will help her make the conscious effort to either make the friendship better or decide to gracefully distance herself.

- **Make T.H.I.N.K. bracelets together.** All you need is a string and five beads of different colors—one for each initial in the anagram THINK. You can both wear the bracelets to remind yourselves to THINK before you text, type, or talk.
- **Just for you: Walk the walk.** As you know, friend drama doesn't end in middle school. While you're teaching your tween to be a better friend, ensure that you're modeling what it looks like to be one yourself. Are you complaining about girlfriends? Gossiping on the phone in clear view of your daughter? It's your job to show her how to treat other women kindly.

The Bottom Line

- Since middle school is the time when girls' greatest influencers shift from their families to their peers, many tweens consider their friendships to be their top priority.

- So much change occurs in a short period of time during middle school, and it's happening to girls at different rates. It's natural for long-time friends to find they no longer have as much in common or to realize they're attracted to new social groups. It's important that girls know it's okay to change.

- As friendships fall apart and come back together, girls can wonder who they can really trust. Since it's so common for girls to feel abandoned or betrayed by their friends, it's vital that they feel safe and loved at home—that they know they can rely on their parents and other caregivers.

- One of the best ways to help your tween deal with friend drama is to encourage her to channel it into being a good friend herself. Strong values like kindness, authenticity and humility aren't naive or weak: they're definite paths to finding and keeping true friends.

CHAPTER SIX

"It's Not Just Cooties Anymore"
Love and Relationships

"In sixth grade, everyone started to be like, 'Have you ever been asked out?' And, 'Have you heard that so-and-so is going out with so-and-so?' I would feel like I was totally out of it, because I wasn't sure how I felt about having a boyfriend. I wasn't really ready for it. I was just kind of confused."

—Taylor, twelve, New York

"I think a lot of the drama at my school is because girls and boys are getting more mature and noticing each other. It's not just cooties anymore."

—Emma, twelve, New Jersey

Girls' friendships change dramatically during middle school, but this is also the time when they become interested in forming other types of relationships—romantic ones. Of course, not all girls will be drawn to boys, but this chapter will focus on this type of attraction for the sake of simplicity.

For me, it all started in fifth grade when a boy in my class, Wes, put a rose in my locker and asked me to go out with him. When I came home and told my mom, she asked me what it meant. "I guess it means I have a boyfriend!" I said excitedly. I remember thinking that as his girlfriend, it was my responsibility to know everything about him—his address, birthday, and favorite things. He sat next to me during recess, and he'd ask about my day, but that was pretty much it. At the time, I didn't worry about what people thought about our relationship, and I didn't stress about how I looked around him or whether he even really liked me.

My first serious crush came in sixth grade. It seemed bigger than my puppy-love romance with Wes. Like everything else during those years, it felt much more *real,* more dramatic. Dustin was older, a seventh grader. I'd known him for years through our church and our town's recreational baseball league. Luckily, he went to a different school, so he was safe to crush on. (If I'd liked someone at my own school, the girls would've watched my every move since inevitably another girl would've liked him too. None of the other girls in my school knew Dustin, so I wasn't stepping on anyone's toes.) Even though I couldn't sing a note, I joined our church youth choir just to be in the same room with him. On Saturday afternoons, my family would cheer for my brother at our community baseball fields, and Dustin's team would often be out warming up at the same time. I thought he was so cute and athletic; I'd beg my mom to let me stay and watch his baseball games. I don't think he even knew I was there!

The next year, word had gotten around: he knew I liked

him, and I thought he liked me too. He'd come over and say hi to me in the stands after his games, lingering around the field, and then he'd load everything up in his mom's car and she'd offer to drive me home. I looked forward to that ride all week: we'd talk about his game, school, his friends, and whatever plans we each had for the rest of the weekend. I spent a *lot* of time getting ready for those Saturday afternoons because I wanted to look just right: cute enough for Dustin but appropriate enough for his mom to approve. Our local mall had just gotten a Bath & Body Works store, and they sold fruity body splashes. I remember carefully choosing the layered tank tops and shorts I'd wear, spraying myself with body splash and wearing lip gloss.

Finally, after what seemed like a lifetime, Dustin sent me an e-mail that said he had thought a lot about it, and he wanted to know if I'd be his girlfriend. I was overjoyed—I'd been crushing on him for so long! I seriously felt as if I'd

High Schoolers Decode: When It All Changed

"In elementary school we were never fascinated by boys. Then you get to middle school and it's like, 'What is this feeling?!' You realize, 'I have a crush on him!' And it's this rush of growing up."

—Brooke, fourteen

won the lottery. He wasn't like any of the other guys I went to school with: he was supersmart, a gentleman who helped out around the church, and didn't seem to care about silly middle school drama. He was such a good guy, in fact, that it didn't weird out my mom at all when I told her I liked him.

What's Going On with Your Middle School Girl and Guys?

From what I've seen over my years at Girl Talk, my Dustin story seems pretty typical for the beginnings of a first relationship. But no matter how your tween is acting around guys, it's probably very normal, since everyone develops at a different rate. My younger sister, for instance, bloomed a few years later than everyone else, which made our three-and-a-half-year difference feel a lot more like five years. (This is a great example of what I've mentioned before about the disparity in maturity among middle schoolers creating a lot of confusion: a girl dreaming about her upcoming sleepover birthday party can be sitting next to a girl who's already sexually active.)

If your tween girl isn't jumping on the boy-crazy bandwagon with her friends, that's okay, and she's not alone. "It just hasn't been time for me," says twelve-year-old Florida seventh grader Sara. "I'm not like, 'Oh, I'm the only one in the world without a boyfriend, life is over.'" Twelve-year-old Emily, in Georgia, can relate—most of the girls in her class are into guys, and she isn't yet. "Girls have started to obsess over guys; they won't stop talking about the guys they like," she says. "I can understand that they'd be interested, but it's still awkward to me because I don't think along those lines. It's like a foreign language. And I'm completely fine with it."

According to a 2008 study released by Liz Claiborne Inc. and LoveIsRespect.org, almost half of tweens—47 percent—do say they've been in a boyfriend-girlfriend relationship, which can be a bit jarring for parents. How can you tell when your daughter's view on boys changes—when she goes from thinking they're annoying to adorable? The same guy she couldn't stand last year, who kept "accidentally" knocking over her desk supplies, making gross fart jokes, and constantly getting in trouble in class for being too loud, is somehow now giving her butterflies. And those butterflies start a chain reaction of changes around how she sees herself, her friends, and boys and how much she shares with you.

For adults, this can seem especially terrifying. Parents often tell us that while they're unsure how to handle the friend drama in their daughters' lives and the new obsessions over personal appearance and materialism, it's this area—boys!—that most concerns them. Their daughter isn't giving them as much detail, and they're not sure what's going on when they're out of view. "I definitely worry about boys; that's their focus now," says Rachel, mom of a middle school girl. "I worry about her not telling me things. Mostly I overhear things when she's talking to her friends, or I'll see that she likes so-and-so."

From what I hear from girls around the country, your fears are probably just that—fears—and the reality is probably not as scary as you might think. I'd guess that whatever your daughter is going through, it probably falls under one of these categories:

- **Not interested.**

  "I have some super-close guy friends, but I don't date that often. I like to have more friends than boyfriends. I'm more concerned with my friendships."

  —Sara, twelve, Florida

- **Interested but not obsessed**

  "I always have a guy that I like—if everybody's talking about boys, I have my say—but when I'm on my own doing my homework, I'm not fantasizing about guys."

  —Jessica, thirteen, New Jersey

- **Wants to meet a guy**

  "With all the crushes and relationships, it's like the whole school is in a giant web and I'm alone. I feel lonely sometimes and depressed. I'd at least like to have a crush or someone I like, but I just don't like any of the guys at my school. There are guys who are cute but are total jerks or are perverted. With a lot of guys at school, I either hate their guts, because they're suddenly turning into jerks, or I know them too well and they're like my brothers."

  —Kalli, eleven, Florida

- **Hopes so . . . someday**

  "I feel a little pressure like, It's got to happen sometime. I think of the Taylor Swift song 'Fifteen' and how she didn't have her first kiss until she was fifteen. I know someday I'll get a boyfriend."

  —Valerie, twelve, Michigan

- **Crushes, but that's it**

  "They go away pretty quickly, to the point where they're not even there, really."

  —Sam, twelve, Washington

- **Boy crazy**

  "When you have a boyfriend, it feels amazing. It's like, 'Wow, we really are connecting.' It's a better feeling than hugging your best friend in the world."

  —Rebecca, thirteen, Texas

Her first crush is so exciting: it's a whole new world of feelings that she hasn't yet experienced. "You blush when he talks to you," twelve-year-old Emily, in Georgia, says of how she feels around boys she likes. "I feel sort of embarrassed sometimes."

Taylor, a New York State seventh grader, speaks to the awkwardness and self-consciousness that accompanies crushes: "You're thinking about every word you're saying. You're constantly thinking, 'I wonder if he thought that was weird.' 'Does this shirt look stupid?' You try to figure out everything they're thinking about."

Once the boy she likes feels the same way, what happens next? Honestly, probably not that much. During middle school, having a boyfriend is more about the title than any potential boyfriend-like activity. "All they do is hold hands and walk around, and it's really awkward because they don't know what to do," says California seventh-grader Charlotte. "By eighth grade, they start acting older, going on dates."

For Tabitha, a New York sixth grader, having a boyfriend seems to be mostly about acting out what she thinks a grown-up relationship would be like:

> *"We text each other sweet texts, like, 'You're pretty,' 'You're cute,' 'I really like you.' I'm not really sure what else you do. When you see each other, you hang out a lot, and eventually, once you're feeling more comfortable with each other, you can kiss and say you love them. But when kids our age say they love each other, they don't really know; it's just that it makes them feel good to say it."*

These changes with boy-girl dynamics don't come without a lot of confusion and, often, heartbreak. Some girls tell me there's a sense of loss during this transition; if they've had a lot of guy friends during elementary school, for example, the added pressure of trying to figure out who likes whom might make them feel less able to freely hang out like they used to. "If you're hanging out with guys, people say you're dating them," says Kalli, eleven, in Florida. "So now my guy friends avoid me. People used to say that my guy friend and I were like siblings, but since they're asking if we're dating, he's stopped talking to me as much."

On the other side of this same spectrum, some girls have realized they've evolved into just-friends material, when they'd like to be seen as a potential girlfriend—which can feel just as painful as losing their guy friends to this new divide. "I'm the friend. The guys talk to me a lot, but if they want to flirt, they'll go to another group," says Hayley, a Washington State seventh grader. "Sometimes I'm not cool with that. I feel like they take advantage of me: 'Oh, we can leave this conversation and talk to other girls; you won't have trouble with that.' But I do."

Across the board, as girls start to expect more from boys—attention, reciprocated feelings—and neither side is sure how to communicate their feelings or what's expected of them, girls report feeling increasingly confused by how guys act. Here are the kinds of things girls say confuse them about guys:

> *"The games they try to play with you. They'll be like, 'Wait on the phone while I talk to someone else.' They see how long they can get you to wait for them, and it's mean."*
>
> —Alex, thirteen, Washington

> *"The way a guy can act so sweet and perfect to you in private, but when he gets in front of his friends or your friends, he acts like a completely different person."*
>
> —Kaitlin, thirteen, Georgia

> *"The way guys talk to you a ton one day and then five minutes later they're talking to another girl a lot. They just switch so easily. And they don't express their emotions; they're not open."*
>
> —Hayley, twelve, Washington

Of course, guys confuse adult women too. But for tween girls, it's the first time they're feeling utterly at a loss around guys' changing personalities and communication style, so they're not sure how to handle it. You might see this conflict as just the beginning of a long road of coming to terms with the disparity between men and women, but to her, it feels a bit like shellshock.

What's the Right Age?

Many of our high schoolers reported that the middle school girls they mentor ask about timing: "They're wondering, When is the right age to start kissing? To have a boyfriend?" sixteen-year-old Dylan told us. "They thought there was a specific age when you should like a guy or have a boyfriend. We tell them it's different for everyone."

Since we all mature at different rates, this is true. My mom didn't make a big deal about my relationship with Dustin; she just told me that if I liked him, then I must have

High Schoolers Look Back: Guys Confused Us Too

"I didn't get their switching of personalities. When you'd see them at school with their friends they'd act differently. It's like, `Why are you doing that?'"

—Alyssa, sixteen

"Girls mature before boys do; they start liking boys, and boys could care less. I was always confused as to why a boy wouldn't want to go on a date or hang out. I wish I'd known back then that boys could still be your friends; I didn't know that until high school and everyone relaxed."

—Brooke, fourteen

good taste in guys ("He's top shelf!" she said). She let it unfold naturally. But a lot of parents place limits for girls—they're not allowed to date or have a boyfriend until they're a specific age.

The tweens I talk to think these rules can be helpful in some ways; age limitations postpone the pressure and keep girls away from the competition to get a boyfriend or give them a good excuse to avoid unwanted attention from boys. Emily, a Georgia twelve-year-old, explains how her mom's rules gave her an easy out: "A good guy friend of mine asked me out. I said, 'I'll tell you tomorrow,' and I talked to my mom about it. She said, 'If you don't want to, you could blame me, and tell him you can't date until you're sixteen.' So I told him that my mom won't allow me to, and we stayed friends."

These limitations can also be a hindrance. By restricting when they're allowed to express their interest in guys, parents can keep girls from maturing at their own rate. They can also shut down potentially important conversations about guys. That's what worries Leni, a middle school mom in New York, and why she lets her sixth grader have boyfriends. "I don't feel like it's something I can prohibit without being lied to," Leni says. "I want her to stay open with me and also develop a track record of healthy relationships. I think by saying, 'You can't date' or 'You can't have a boyfriend,' I'd shut down those conversations." This is exactly why thirteen-year-old Bridget doesn't talk to her parents about guys: they've placed age restrictions on her that make her feel as if she can't bring up the subject. "There are things I've always wanted to ask my mom, but if I ever mention guys, she's like, 'Not until you're sixteen!' and shrugs it off," says Bridget. "So I talk to my friends about guys."

This is exactly why I always advise middle school parents to *listen* when their tween girls are talking. Maybe you feel the way Bridget's mom does: there's no point in discussing this because you've told her she can't date until high school (it seems more likely that her mom is uncomfortable with the topic and is just hoping to avoid it). Or maybe it's just that you're superbusy at that moment. But if she feels that she can't talk to you, she'll find someone who *will* listen to her, and you might not know what that person is suggesting or advising—another reason that giving her an adopted older sister to talk to is incredibly important.

High Schoolers Look Back: I Had to Wait Until Sixteen

I'm grateful, but it was hard . . .

"I didn't like my parents' rule at the time. But when I broke up with my boyfriend recently, it was very hard; I was crying every night, and I'm glad my thirteen-year-old self was spared that heartbreak. I think it was easier to talk to my parents about guys because of the rule, too, because it prevented drama. And it keeps you focused on your own life when you're younger. . . . Still, I was really angry when everyone was texting their boyfriends and I had no one to text. Or everyone's boyfriend was coming to the game, but I never had anyone to sit with at the game. They'd be like, 'Me and John went to the movies.' All I did was stay home."

—Imani, sixteen

When tweens say they don't want to talk to their parents about guys, what they usually mean is that they don't want to talk to them about sex. "Parents think that having a conversation may lead to something else, like their daughters having sex, but it's not even like that," says eighteen-year-old Kendall, one of Girl Talk's high school mentors. "Girls just want someone to talk to."

That's true. I often think parents assume the worst, when in fact, just having a first kiss is still a huge deal. I know it was to me. There was so much drama about whether Dustin and I were going to kiss that it ended up hurting our relationship. By the summer after my seventh-grade year, we were definitely a couple. We'd only been together for a few months, and I was starting to feel bummed because he was about to start high school, leaving me behind in middle school. He was actually going to transfer to my school (it went from sixth to twelfth grade), but he'd be in ninth grade, so he'd be surrounded by gorgeous older girls, and I'd have to watch from afar, still in eighth grade. I considered Dustin the best-kept secret in town, but now he'd no longer be a secret.

At least we had that summer—or so I thought, until Dustin's friends got in the way. Even though they were just a year older, his group seemed light-years ahead of my class. We'd hear rumors about his friends hooking up with girls, and half of the time we didn't even understand their terminology or know what the rumors meant. I felt safe with Dustin, though; for one thing, he was a total gentleman, a really good guy who wasn't at all the type to pressure me into anything physical. And he was kind of a late bloomer, a relief when compared to his older-seeming guy friends.

But his friends obviously wanted to make sure Dustin

was at their level. One day that summer, he was over at my house watching a movie. My parents and siblings were home (I wasn't allowed to be alone in the house with boys), and after the movie was over, we walked outside. As we stood under the carport talking, Dustin suddenly leaned over to try and kiss me. *Oh no!* I thought. *I'm not ready! And definitely not when my parents might see us!* On instinct, I moved my head to the side, so he ended up kissing me on the cheek—*awkward.* But I had the sense that maybe he wasn't ready either, that he was just doing it to get his friends to leave him alone.

For the next few days, things were okay, and it didn't seem that our kissing fiasco had changed anything. There was a church retreat at the beach that weekend, and I was psyched—I knew it would be my last chance to really get quality time with Dustin before school started. But during that trip, one of Dustin's friends walked up to me: "Heard you gave Dustin the 'duck and weave,'" he said. "Huh?" I asked. "What do you mean?" He smirked and walked off, leaving me standing there, confused. The duck and weave?

I knew he was somehow referring to our failed kiss. After that, I wasn't too surprised when Dustin broke up with me before the weekend was over. I cried and cried on the ride home. I'd liked him for *so* long and now he actually was coming to my school; all the girls would find out and make fun of me—and, of course, try to date him. Had they all had their first kisses? I had no idea. I felt lost without someone to confide in, and this was way too awkward to talk to my mom about.

When I got home from the trip, I got on Instant Messenger to tell Maryashley what happened. Dustin was on Instant Messenger too. "I'm really sorry it went down that way," he typed. Then his demeanor changed, and I knew his friend had jumped on Dustin's account: "Haley, we all know you're great, but Dustin is going to be in high school," his friend typed. "He needs a girl who's not going to pull back."

Yikes. Hearing that just made it all worse. I definitely felt like I'd messed it up. I kept asking myself: *Why didn't you kiss him?* And then answering myself: *But I wasn't ready!*

Of course, now I'm proud that I made that decision. There wouldn't have been anything wrong if the stars had aligned and it felt comfortable and right to me, but at that point, I wasn't emotionally ready. I'd envisioned my first kiss to be something special, like out of a movie.

During that bus ride home from our church retreat, I really, really wished I had an older sister. As much as I loved my mom and as supportive as she'd been through all my school drama thus far, this was one situation when it would've been way easier to confide in someone else.

These boy issues might be the most crucial time for an adopted older sister to have a positive effect on your middle school girl. Although girls at this age have different perspectives on guys and dating, they almost unanimously say that they don't feel comfortable completely confiding in their parents around relationships and sexuality.

I'd be willing to bet that if the middle school girl in your life is in a relationship, your imagination is much worse than the reality. If you've read her texts and see that she's had her first kiss, or you overhear her on the phone saying, "I love you, too," to her puppy-love boyfriend, you might think: teen pregnancy! Sexting! Dating abuse! *She's too young to date, let alone be "in love,"* you might think. Your mind goes from A to Z instead of A to B.

But despite the stories we hear about how kids are developing sexually so much sooner than ever before and how they're constantly bombarded by sexual images in the media, there's still probably no need to freak out. For one, kids do listen to their parents. In her book *The Real Truth about Teens and Sex*, in which she surveyed over 1,000 teens, author Sabrina Weill points out repeatedly that your children *do* internalize the messages you send them about sex. (You have to be careful what messages you're sending!)

Second, remember that for tweens, a kiss is most likely just that—it's a huge deal in and of itself. It's not the first step that it is for adults. Having her first kiss won't necessarily lead down some slippery slope to sexual experimentation. For most tweens and teens, becoming sexually active is still very much a step-by-step process, not a huge all-in-one leap.

And finally, no matter what you're reading or the terrible stories you've heard, you know your child better than anyone else does. If she's sneaking out and visiting boys in the middle of the night or is just having her first kiss, you're probably in tune with that. Check out the next box to see how tweens characterize their sexual activity in middle school.

Girls Talk:
Are People at School Hooking Up?

"A lot of moms think 'hooking up' means sex. In my school, 'hooking up' means kissing with tongue."

—Jessica, thirteen, New Jersey

"Couples don't even hug at our school. It's kind of a relief because there's no pressure, and if I don't want to go far, I'd feel secure saying no."

—Kaitlin, thirteen, Georgia

"I haven't kissed my boyfriends, and if they're going to be my boyfriend, they have to respect that. I do want to sometimes. But if someone catches you, it could hurt your reputation in high school."

—Rebecca, thirteen, Texas

"If you're dating, you're expected to make out. There's a lot of people fingering and giving blow jobs. Knowing what other people are doing makes me realize my boundaries more than I feel like I would have otherwise. The downside is that a lot of girls will get really bad reputations afterward and guys don't."

—Alex, thirteen, Washington

"When I had my first boyfriend, I was really nervous. I didn't know what to do. I asked my friends, 'What should I say? Should I just be myself?' I Googled 'how to kiss a guy' because it was too awkward to ask my mom or friends. Google and Yahoo! Answers were there for me."

—Charlotte, twelve, California

Talking about Boys, Sex, and Relationships

Here's what you *might* want to say: "You're my baby girl! You can't be talking/thinking/asking about this!" But if you do that, you automatically undermine whatever your middle school girl is going through, leading her to mistrust you and feel hurt and unheard. She'll want to feel both normal and validated by you.

And you don't want to slam the door on these conversations. She won't think you're a potential source of information, and she'll seek answers from someone else—and who knows who that could be. "Parents would be so appalled by the thought of your having sex that they wouldn't understand it if you wanted to talk about it," explains Alex, a thirteen-year-old in Florida. "Friends will help you understand your feelings, and help you not do anything stupid. Parents would just say NO. They wouldn't talk about the good things and bad things; they'd just say NO WAY. They'll judge you."

Rebecca, a Texan eighth grader, says she has a superclose relationship with her mom, but still avoids this subject for precisely the same reasons. "I tell my mom if I'm dating someone or not, but I don't go into depth about it because she's awkward," she says. "If I told her I kissed someone, she'll be like, 'What?! No!' She knows I'm not going to do anything 'bad,' but if I say, 'He gave me a hug today' or 'He held my hand,' she'll be awkward around me for days. So now I keep that stuff to myself."

Even if it's uncomfortable for you, as it is for Rebecca's mom or for Bridget's mom earlier in this chapter, wouldn't you rather your middle school girl learn about relationships and sex from you? Isn't it safer to get over your own fears and discomfort so that your daughter doesn't repress her questions, like Rebecca, or turn to someone you don't know?

Staying calm and casual ("Hey, is there anything you'd like to talk about?") seems to work for the girls we know. It's also incredibly powerful for girls when you share your own experiences: "This is what it was like for me. I know it might be different for you, but I just thought I'd tell you what it was like for me."

Here are more ways to make it easier for your daughter to open up about guys:

Don't tease.

No matter how cute you think her puppy love is, if you mercilessly bug her about it (or, more likely, if a father/step-father/older brother/uncle does), she's more likely to think that you don't get it and shut you out. "If I'd say something about thinking a guy was cute, they'd get mushy, and that makes you feel awkward," eighteen-year-old Ashley, a high school mentor, recalls. "If they were cooler about it, that would've helped."

Stay calm: don't jump to conclusions or freak out.

"I didn't talk to my parents in middle school because I thought they'd be like, 'You're too young,' and they wouldn't trust me," fourteen-year-old Heidi says. "I wished they'd been calmer so I could talk to them."

Tell her your own middle school stories.

"If moms talked about their middle school experiences, it would make their daughters feel more comfortable," advises Britney, a sixteen-year-old Girl Talk Leader. "My neighbor had all these stories about being cheated on in middle school and high school, realizing that she'd find someone who would love her for who she is—and I think hearing her stories made me feel like I wasn't alone."

Don't warn without an explanation.

"When I was in sixth grade, I had a crush on an older guy," says Hayley, twelve, from Washington. "My mom didn't like him. She'd say, 'You need to watch out.' I didn't know what she meant, and I was annoyed that she wasn't seeing that I was happy. I would've understood if she'd said, 'Here are the reasons why I'm worried.' I probably wouldn't have listened completely or changed anything—but I would've known where she was coming from."

**Let her confide in someone you trust
(find that adopted older sister!).**

"I talk to my older step-cousin about guys," says thirteen-year-old Bridget in New Jersey. "She's protective, but doesn't freak out. I didn't know what to say to a guy I like, and she said to just be cool, say hi, ask about homework, talk about a teacher. And it worked."

When It Gets Tough

Along with the first crush, first butterflies, first boyfriend, and first kiss comes the first heartbreak. Middle school girls might not experience the major heartbreak they'll probably deal with later on, but even so, feeling rejected at any age *hurts*. The way Dustin and I broke up felt so wrong, because I knew he didn't really want to and that he'd just caved to the pressure. I cried for days, and even by the time school started that fall, it still hurt to see the ninth-grade girls crushing on him and to worry about running into him in the hallways. And I felt so alone: I hadn't yet met Christie, and I didn't feel that I could talk to anyone who'd really get it. Max, a thirteen-year-old in Florida, seems to understand how I felt: "It's not a broken heart unless the person means as much to you as life itself. And that's how much my ex-boyfriend meant to me. He made me so happy."

For girls who instigate a breakup, though, it can be an opportunity to realize what you'd like a relationship to be like—and what you don't:

"I recently dumped this guy who was nice to me but really rude to other people. I envisioned growing old with him and was like, 'No, I'm not going to do that.' If you're dumping them for the right reasons, it gives you self-respect. It's like preparing myself for the real world. I want someone who's going to be respectful and say nice things instead of bad things."

—Rebecca, thirteen, Texas

Just-Been-There Advice:
What We Know about Heartache

We dealt with it too

"This boy and I decided to go out. We were at a party—the first time we'd gone out in public since becoming a couple—when a friend came up to me and said she'd seen him kissing another girl. I was so hurt."

—Brooke, fourteen

"I had a crush on my best guy friend. It was heartbreaking to like someone and to have them not like you back. I remember crying and playing Mariah Carey's 'We Belong Together' a lot."

—Kendall, eighteen

There's always another guy

"I tell the girls I work with, 'There are only a certain number of people at this school. Once you get to high school, who knows who'll you'll meet.'"

—Kanisha, twenty-one

"In middle school it seems like there are five boys, and one of them has to like you, and it's your job to make that happen—but it's not."

—Grace, eighteen

"Girls think that these are the only guys that they're going to see. They're thinking, 'If I don't go out with this guy now, I never will, and if I don't have a boyfriend now, I never will.'"

—Britney, sixteen

My anchor activity, volunteering at the literacy center, and my relationship with Christie kept me busy so my mind was less occupied with boys, but there's something else I had that can help all girls: I had some awesome older men in my life, men who emulated the kind of guy I'd ultimately want to be with. My relationships with my dad, my grandfather (aka "Papa"), and a family friend named Parks, who'd already raised his two amazing daughters, played big roles in my life when it came to guys.

I've focused on the importance of having an adopted older sister, and that's still vitally important here because she can help a middle school girl decode boys' confusing mixed messages and can console and relate to your middle schooler. But in my work, I've seen that having some dependable, responsible, and loving men around—a father, a father-like figure, or both—can make a huge difference to a middle school girl. When I look back and wonder how I made good choices about guys, I think it all comes down to seeing how these men acted, how they modeled respectful behavior. My grandfather opened the car door for his wife; I wanted a guy who'd do that too. He'd take me out to lunch and tell me how proud he was of me, which was especially helpful during those years when I felt like I was never good enough for my classmates. Parks was like an uncle to me; he and his wife would come to my dance recitals or take me out to lunch and ask, with all sincerity, how I was doing. (It's also really helpful to have a safe male perspective on boys' behavior.) Because of their influence, I knew I wanted a man like my awesome and supportive husband, Paul—

High Schoolers Look Back: How Parents Helped with Heartbreak

My mom told me to listen to my heart

"I told my mom when my boyfriend cheated on me. She said, 'Listen to your heart.' I asked her, 'How can I do that?' She said, 'If you get a twinge inside, or a feeling that something isn't right, or he pressures you, back out of the situation. He has no right to tell you to do something you're not comfortable with, and there's nothing wrong with leaving if he's not treating you the way he should.'"

—Brooke, fourteen

They lift me up

"If a guy hurts me, they tell me all of the good things about me—that I'm beautiful and any guy would be lucky to have me. It really helps."

—Annie, eighteen

who really mirrors the respectful behavior I saw in my dad, my grandfather, and Parks.

With more and more single-parent families, it's especially important to make sure your middle school girl has a strong male presence in her life. And it doesn't have to be weird or uncomfortable. Just like you can seek out an adopted older sister for her, you can seek out an older male presence—a coach, a family friend, a youth minister, whatever. Someone you can trust to have your daughter's best interests at heart, someone you can e-mail and say, "Hey, my daughter's dealing with such-and-such. Could you talk to her?" Ask her uncle to congratulate her on making the honor roll; ask a teacher to keep an eye out at school. To this day, my grandfather and I have regular lunch dates just as we did throughout school—and it's still empowering to me to hear him say that I've made him proud.

Try This: Help Her Know What to Expect

- **Take her on a mother-daughter date.** Take her out to her favorite restaurant, followed by a game of miniature golf, or walk around a local park. This is a perfect time to talk about your experiences with guys, both good and bad. Encourage your daughter to tell you what she wants in a guy.
- **Have a "rom-com" night.** Spend a weekend evening watching a few romantic comedies together. Analyze the characters. What qualities are admirable in the male and

female leads? Which ones aren't? What messages about love and romantic expectations do the movies offer, and are these realistic? What would your daughter do in the same situation? Use the issues the movies bring up as a way to start a discussion with your daughter around love and relationships.

The Bottom Line

- Girls are developing at vastly different rates, so crushing on a guy can mean a variety of things. Girls can feel insecure about being left behind if it seems that everyone else is boy crazy. Increased attention to boys can often mean that her relationships with girlfriends will change.

- Having a boyfriend and experiencing her first kiss doesn't mean that sexual activity is immediately the next step. Trust that she has internalized what you've taught her.

- Heartbreak can be a way for her to learn what kind of relationship she wants in the future.

- Although there are ways to encourage your tween to open up to you more, most girls say they don't want to talk to their parents about guys. Giving her an adopted older sister to talk to will allow her to have someone trustworthy to confide in.

182

CHAPTER SEVEN

Dealing with *You*

Getting Along with Parents

"Instead of, 'Mom, look at that stuffed animal I want!' it's more like, 'Mom, I need a new bra size.'"

—Rebecca, thirteen, Texas

I've always been really close with my parents, but my conversations with them changed once I started middle school. Although I wanted them to support and comfort me, I didn't want them to think I still needed elementary school–style babying or to restrict my freedom because they were worried about me. In a way, I thought that confiding in them less would protect them from worrying about all the drama.

Even within a strong parent-daughter relationship, there's a natural disconnect that happens in middle school. It's a normal part of growing up: your tween is on her own more now, hanging around older kids, and she has more independence, freedom, and responsibility. She no longer needs nonstop adult supervision, so you're not with her as much as you might've been during her elementary years.

And even if she's constantly chatting as soon as she gets in the car after school or over dinner, you're probably still wondering what she's *not* telling you.

You'd be right to suspect that your tween is not confiding in you about all the aspects of her life. Over and over, girls tell me that they share less with their parents once they're in middle school. "I don't tell her about my relationship problems, and the fights that I have with my friends," says Courtney, a twelve-year-old in New Jersey. "I definitely have more of a private life now." Max, a thirteen-year-old Florida tween, says that she saw a shift happen from sixth grade, when she still told her parents everything, to her current eighth-grade strategy. Now, she says, "I talk to my mom only if it's really important." Like most other girls, she has started to rely more on her friends. Part of her reluctance to share comes from the generation gap, she says: "Your parents were in this situation ten, twenty, thirty years ago; they don't really know what it's like in this age. Friends are going through the same things, so they understand more."

This doesn't mean that your tween is hiding from you. She's just being more careful with what she chooses to tell you. "There are some things I would tell them all about before, and now I'm not as open to telling them," says Jessie, a Georgia eighth grader. "It's not *that* different, I just don't go as in depth, or I talk around things."

So what is she not telling you? As you could guess from the previous chapter, the number-one off-limits topic is boys. She's worried you'll judge her and shut down the conversation—she doesn't want to hear that automatic *no* whenever she brings up the topic. "If I ask if I can have a party with a couple of guys, they'll say, 'No way,'" says Bridget, thirteen, in New Jersey. "They act like something bad is going to happen. If I go to the roller rink, the first question is, 'Are there any boys going?'" So she's learned not to bring up guys at all.

If your tween is feeling a lot of pressure from you about school and is worried she might disappoint you, then she'll clam up when asked about that topic too. Elena, a thirteen-year-old in Washington, says she doesn't tell her mom about tests or quizzes because "I'm already stressed, and her pressuring me to study will just make it worse. She'll be like, 'Did you study, did you study?!' And I don't need that before a test." Instead, she'll tell her mom about it afterward.

Most girls say that friend drama is one of the main topics they *do* confide in their parents about—unless they think it might change their parents' perception of their friends or provoke questions they might not want to answer about their social situations. "If I said, 'I'm really mad at so and so,' the next day that'd be over with, but they'd still ask me about it and wonder why it's okay that I'm still friends with her," explains Hillary, an eighth grader in Georgia. "I think if they knew, they'd unintentionally make it last longer."

Sometimes these girls feel that they don't even know what they can talk to adults about. They honestly aren't sure, so they're testing the waters. Hayley, a Washington State seventh grader, describes this ambivalence; she also touches on another topic that girls say is off-limits: any family drama.

"I don't know exactly what to tell them anymore. If I tell them something about school, it might turn into a lecture. When it comes to boys or certain friends' problems, I don't tell them because I don't know if I can trust them. I don't think I can tell them how I feel about our relationship at home: they might get mad, and we wouldn't end up talking about it."

Of course, there are lots of superclose families, and many girls who say they still tell their parents everything. Even if you have that kind of relationship with your daughter, there is some wisdom to gain from the girls in this chapter. As you probably know by now, middle school girls easily shut down if they feel a situation isn't safe to discuss or if they won't be heard; without even realizing it, you could say something that might make her less likely to share with you. (We'll be tackling arguments, family fighting, rules, and boundaries in the next chapter.)

So why didn't I confide completely in my mom? It might seem strange, since I've told you lots of anecdotes of times

High Schoolers Look Back: We Dealt with It Too

"I was afraid that by sharing with them, I'd move toward elementary school rather than high school. Sometimes you want to test things out before you go tell your parents, like changing friend groups. You want to make your own mistakes and decisions rather than having them guide you all the time."

—Alyssa, sixteen

"I wished I could talk to them, but I didn't know how to approach them."

—Heidi, fourteen

I poured my heart out to her. I certainly shared some of the friend drama with my parents, but I didn't tell them all of it (which led to that disastrous cookie cake birthday incident I told you about earlier!). I think it's because I didn't want them to wonder what was wrong with me. I didn't want them to think I'd done something that prompted the other girls not to invite me to parties or to treat me badly. Instead of that comforting, "Oh they're just jealous," or "They're feeling insecure too," I was afraid of hearing them say, "Well, what have you done?" Since I was already worrying myself with these questions, I certainly didn't want to hear it from them too. Would they blame me, or would they always, no matter what, be on my side? From what

High Schoolers Look Back:
We Should've Talked to Our Parents More

"I never wanted to get too close to my mom, to break that boundary of mom and kid. I didn't want to change her opinion of me. It was especially hard around school; my parents would always say, 'You're so smart,' so when I would do badly, I thought their view of me as smart would change. Looking back, I don't understand why I cared so much—I knew they'd love me no matter what I made on a test. They'd just know that I didn't try as hard as I should have."

—Ashley, eighteen

I've seen with girls all over the country, I think my experience of holding back is pretty universal. Everything is in so much flux at this time that most girls aren't sure how they'll be perceived by their parents—because they're not even sure how they perceive themselves. They haven't formed a strong enough sense of self yet to deal with any of these assumptions about how parents might respond.

These girls also don't think their parents could possibly understand what they're going through. Middle schoolers have felt this way forever. I remember saying to my mom, "You have no idea what I'm going through on IM! You didn't have the Internet." And she'd say, "Girls were still just as hurtful: they'd write mean things on your car; they'd call and hang up on you. I do understand." Though this did offer me a measure of comfort, it still didn't feel like she could really get what it felt like to be attacked online. Plus, even if she did go through the same thing, it happened so long ago—just like Max mentioned earlier.

At the time, I was also trying to protect my parents, too. In a way, I didn't want them to understand the full scope of what was happening and how mean those girls were, because I wanted to spare them the embarrassment of knowing the truth about how I was treated at school—I also didn't want them to tell me never to talk to those girls again or to never use Instant Messenger. I liked the social outlet provided by IM, but if they knew how much it was a source of pain for me, they might tell me to delete my account.

When girls tell me why they're suddenly more hesitant to share with their parents, they cite similar reasons. Just as I did, they're afraid of having their very precious and, to them, hard-won freedom restricted. As eleven-year-old Florida sixth grader Kalli says: "We're getting into more fights, which means I'll open up less. I'm always careful about what I say so I don't get into more trouble. I'm worried that she won't understand and then I wouldn't have as much freedom."

On a similar note, they're concerned that what might start out as a simple conversation with you could turn into something much larger, with possible repercussions. If they've made a mistake and turn to the adults in their lives for advice, will they get in trouble? "When I hit middle school, I couldn't talk to my parents about wanting to go out with a guy because I knew I'd get in trouble," recalls Bridget, the New Jersey thirteen-year-old. "I knew they'd turn the conversation around and it'd probably turn into a fight. If you try to stand up for yourself, they'll just ground you."

There's a power dynamic here, of course. As a parent, you're in charge; she's still living under your rules and your supervision. As she gains more freedom to make her own mistakes, sharing with you could come at a price. She's afraid she'll be punished for telling the truth if it's something you don't want to hear—if she got a bad grade, for example, or got in trouble at school, or even if she shares with you that she's angry about family dynamics at home. Girls don't want their parents to get mad at them, punish them, or lecture them.

Sometimes tweens aren't sure how parents will react—but they don't want to find out, so it's easier to keep quiet. "My mom gets mad if I don't tell her things, but it seems like she gets mad if I do too," says Elena, a Washington thirteen-year-old. "I hate that, because I feel like I should be talking to my mom. But what's the point of telling her when I'm going to get a reaction that's not helpful? It would defeat the purpose since I'm already upset."

Beneath the threat of repercussions from sharing with parents and adults lies a deeper fear for tweens: that their parents' perception of them will change or that their parent-child relationship will be disrupted. Thirteen-year-old Alex in Washington says that though she knows her mom is hurt that she doesn't tell her everything anymore, she feels that she doesn't have a choice. "There's stuff I can't tell her because it would ruin our relationship," she says. "Like information about a friend I don't want her to know because she won't want me hanging out with that person."

Girls spend so much time at this age concerned about how they'll be judged. From Chapter 2, you know that part of their increased stress stems from feeling like they can't make a mistake—that love and acceptance only come from being perfect. They're taught to be pleasers from an early age, and if they've grown up receiving all the gold stars and pats on the back, they might think that your love is conditional—that they'll only be accepted if they're "good" girls. "My parents have very high expectations, so I worry about telling them stuff," says Alex. "If I say, 'Oh, my friend kissed this guy,' they'll say, 'I hope you would never do that.' I'm like, 'Okay, but it's obviously going to happen eventually.' They can be very judgmental sometimes, and that makes it really hard for me to be able to talk to them about stuff."

The idea that girls might do, or say, or try something while they're growing up that flies in the face of what you know about them is too much for them to bear. What's easier? Not telling you at all. And it serves multiple purposes: they get to have a private life while your opinion of them remains untarnished. So although they'd often like to share with you more, they're scared about your reaction. "I'm worried that she might judge me or see me differently," New Jersey native Kelly, thirteen, says about why she holds back from her mom. "I want to tell her, but once you do, it's like, 'Oh, what else is my child doing?'"

How Do You Gain Her Trust?

Honestly, even if you want her to, your middle school girl *shouldn't* be telling you everything. Girls at this age are growing up and establishing identities separate from their families; deciding what to share with you and what to keep for themselves is a natural, healthy, and normal part of entering into adolescence. (Ideally your tween will be sharing with an adopted older sister who can help her through all the things she's not telling you.)

But there's a lot you can do to make sure she feels comfortable coming to you when she does want and need to. From my work with girls, I've found a few things that can help make it easier for you to form these bonds:

Make time.

It might sound overly obvious, but many adults need to be reminded to do this. Many of our middle schoolers feel that their parents are just too busy or distracted with work, juggling domestic responsibilities, or their personal lives, to be there for them. "Before around 8:30 at night, my parents are always only half listening because they're working and their e-mails are always dinging," says Hillary, a thirteen-year-old in Georgia. Charlotte, a twelve-year-old California girl, feels the same about her mom: "She seems too busy with her job to be able to be there for me sometimes." Even though my parents were almost always there for me, they see that they could've listened more. Now they realize that cutting the grass and working on home projects might not have been as important as sitting down and talking with their kids.

Let her experiment.

If your daughter wants to get her hair highlighted, wear all black, or kiss a boy in a bathroom, it's doesn't mean that rehab is the next step. Getting a henna tattoo on spring break won't automatically turn her into Courtney Love (she probably won't even remember she wanted a henna tattoo on spring break!). It's all part of her journey toward figur-

High Schoolers Look Back:
My Mom Wasn't Around

"Sometimes it felt like my mom wasn't completely there in the conversation. My sister and I would talk to her about school, and she'd give brief answers; she didn't really seem like she was completely engaged. I definitely felt like I was being pushed aside. It hurt my feelings: What was going on in her life that preempted getting closer to us?"

—Britney, sixteen

ing out who she is, of finding her own way. She needs to be able to experiment around you. Tabitha appreciates that her mother lets her express herself. "It's not that she doesn't care what I do, but she lets me have freedom," the eleven-year-old New Yorker says. "She's not uptight, like 'You can't paint your nails.' She let me get my ears pierced. She taught me how to put on eyeliner. She's very mellow."

Just listen.

At times throughout middle school, I remember feeling that my parents and I weren't communicating. Because of something that had happened earlier in the day, I'd come home and be short with my parents, or with my brother and sister—when really, I was hurting and needed to talk to someone. My parents would send me to my room, and I'd end up crying there until I fell asleep. I always hoped that one of them would come in and say, "What are you going through? Let's talk about it. I know this is something deeper than bumping your sister in the spaghetti line." You don't want to punish your girl for being short; you want her to come in and talk about the reason she's acting this way. Bridget shares her frustrations that her parents don't really listen, while Charlotte is grateful she has her dad's support:

"My parents only listen to what they want to listen to. Once you really start pouring your heart out to them, they'll interrupt you and say what they think is best. When my mom asks why I don't talk to her as much, I want to say, 'Because you interrupt me!' But I don't want to start an argument."
—Bridget, thirteen, New Jersey

"I talk to my dad a lot; we have heart-to-heart conversa-
tions, with crying involved. I'll just say, 'Dad, can we talk?'
A lot of parents say, 'Oh, I have to work.' Even though he
has to work, he still makes time. We'll go into a room and
he sits there, and is quiet, and listens. Then he'll give me all
these options. I end up picking one of them."

—Charlotte, twelve, California

Don't tell your tween's secrets.

When girls see you huddling with other parents in a carpool line, they can easily make assumptions: What are you

High Schoolers Look Back: My Parents Made It Easy

"In middle school, I just told them what they had to
know—like where I was going to be after school and the
main details of my life. Now I tell them practically everything. Even if I mess up, like getting in trouble at school,
I'll tell them. They're unique because they work together as
a team to make it comfortable for me to talk to them: everything is game, even things like alcohol, and they make it
okay to talk about those things just by bringing them up.
Plus, they genuinely care about who I am and who I want
to be, and they want to help me get there. They love me no
matter what. I can't really say that about my friends."

—Imani, sixteen

telling them? If you're friends with other moms and your middle schooler thinks you're talking about her to them, she's much less likely to share with you because she doesn't know if she can trust you. "She's overly involved in mom gossip, and I don't know if I can trust her to keep my secrets safe," says Courtney, a New Jersey twelve-year-old. "If I tell her something, I'm afraid she'll tell her friends. Sometimes they drive me home and mention things I've told my mom in confidence, and I feel like 'Oh, okay, I can't trust her anymore.' It doesn't feel good. I want to be able to completely trust my mom." You might think it's harmless (or even a way to form your own bonds with other moms, or add to your own social status), but to your daughter, it's not okay.

This is true even within your own family. If she tells you

Just-Been-There Advice:
I Told My Mom What I Needed

"Girls may not want to tell their parents because they'll overreact. In one situation, I went to my mom and said, 'I just want you to listen'—and she did. It helped a lot to first create an understanding between us of what kind of communication I wanted. It's natural to stop sharing—all of my friends have gone through it with their mothers—but if girls let parents know that they just want them to listen, it makes a huge difference."

—Heidi, fourteen

something in confidence, don't talk about it with her siblings (or even your partner or her other parent, if she asks you to and it's safe not to). She'll know when you break her trust, like Jessica, a New Jersey thirteen-year-old: "All the girls in my family are big gossipers. Sometimes my mom will announce, 'Jessica's crying!' I don't need people to know that. I don't want to be embarrassed."

Get personal (but don't be besties).

Transparency and honesty go a long way with middle schoolers, as Tabitha, a New York sixth grader, says: "She's very honest with me. When I asked her how babies were made, she told it to me flat out, right there. She didn't lie to me and I liked that, because I didn't grow up being clueless.

High Schoolers Look Back:
We Worried about Mom Gossip Too

"My school was a small private school, and everyone was always together at these different functions, so moms were bound to share information, like, 'Who's your kid's best friend?' I know she'd never mean to talk about who I was mad at, but sometimes she'd slip and say things I didn't want her to say. Moms might not know that what they're sharing is potentially hurtful to their daughters."

—Alyssa, sixteen

I've asked her lots of questions about growing up, and she answers them. She's very willing to tell me stuff."

Sharing something about yourself, or your past, lets her know that you trust her as much as she trusts you. This way she won't feel as vulnerable with her secrets. Hayley wishes her parents would open up more about their own lives. "I think it might help if my parents talked to me more about things that were going on with them," says the Washington seventh grader. "I feel like we all need to update each other on how we are. If they shared more, I'd feel more comfortable sharing with them."

Still, girls don't need another best friend; they need a parent. A great middle school mom might have a lot of the characteristics of a friend, but ultimately, you're the guardrail, the safety net, in her life.

I've seen relationships fall into trouble because the mom tries too hard to be the "cool mom" or BFFs with her daughter. This seems to happen more often with moms who have a lot of free time and are trying to relive their adolescence through their daughters, or divorced moms who might be competing with their ex's "cool" new girlfriend or wife. Sure, it's flattering to hear your daughter say, "My mom is my best friend!" But you don't necessarily want that, since it can be too dangerous when it's time to discipline your daughter or set boundaries.

High Schoolers Look Back:
So Glad My Mom Shared

"My mom made it really clear that she'd rather know and be prepared than to not know and have something horrible happen. When I had my first kiss when I was thirteen—she'd previously told me about hers, so I wasn't scared that it wasn't okay or taboo. I knew her story, and it was a moment rather than being embarrassing or weird."

—Grace, eighteen

"My mom was very open with us since childhood, so I felt like she knew me inside and out. It cleared the way for us to be open with her. We never felt like she was hiding herself or her life from us."

—Kanisha, twenty-one

Watch your words.

You know how I wanted my parents to come in and talk to me when I was crying in my room? I think every girl wants that. Sometimes I'd have a bad day and scream, "I just want to be left alone!" Of course, what I really wanted was for my mom to give me a hug and say, "Okay"—but instead, she'd snap back and say, "You're such a brat!" or "No wonder those girls think you're snobby!" Ouch. I knew that she was frustrated and stressed out, but at the time, I was just shocked: *You're my mom!* I'd think. *You're not supposed to say hurtful things! You're supposed to just hug me and tell me that everything will be okay.*

This can be a frustrating reality for parents, but it's the truth. For all the times that you are comforting and loving and supportive, your girl will remember the *one* time that you say something you'll regret. As important as it is to love her through these years by trying to be supportive and compassionate, it's equally important to try *not* to say things that could wound her. Thirteen-year-old Kaitlin in Georgia describes how painful it is to be knocked down verbally by her mom:

> *"One time when she was mad at me, she said, 'You're a sorry excuse for an idiot.' The sharp things she says put me down, and I remember every little bit of them. They're*

High Schoolers Look Back: Mom Shut Us Out

"We'd see our mom leaving, and she'd be like, 'I'm going out,' without telling us where. We'd feel abandoned—why can't you tell us, exactly? I really felt shut out of my mom's life. I definitely think it would've been better if she hadn't hid her own life, but I don't know if she knows how to do that—or if she'd be willing."

—Britney, sixteen

very hurtful. That phrase, 'Sticks and stones will break my bones'—that's a lie. Words hurt really bad. I get scared when she loses her patience that she'll take it out on me by snapping at me. I definitely can't stand up to her because I'll get in trouble. She has everything over me. I just feel like I need to be as humble as I can and just move on and try my best to ignore it. After a fight I'll just go to my room and sit and on my bed and think about what she said and start to cry. It really sinks in. She definitely doesn't apologize: she's always right, so why should she?"

Don't use her words against her.

If she tells you something in confidence, let her know that you won't use it against her in the future or throw it back in her face. "I don't want what I said to come back and haunt me," says Kelly, an eighth grader in New Jersey. "I know the moment we're sharing is great, but later if we have a fight, she might bring it up and snap it back at me. If you say something and you wish you hadn't, it's there and can't be erased."

Often girls want to share with parents during a close moment, but they wonder if it's safe. *If I tell them this now,* they think, *what will happen when this moment is over and my parents are back to being in charge?* What if you get in an argument the next day? Will you abuse her confidence? Courtney has a story about this. "Once I told her about this time when I lied to my friend," says the New Jersey twelve-year-old. "Later she brought it back up when we were fighting—she was like, 'Well, you lied to your best friend, so . . .' It made me feel bad about myself. I was opening up and being vulnerable and she used it against me."

Besides gaining her trust and talking to her more, here are more things girls say they want from their parents:

What Girls Want Their Parents to Do

- ### Cheer them up
  "When I've had a really bad day at school, I wish she'd say 'Let's go do something fun,' instead of, 'Let's go home and do homework.' Even just going through the drive-through and getting an iced tea together; it doesn't take a lot to make me happy. Going straight to homework just makes me more depressed after a long day."
  —Rebecca, thirteen, Texas

- ### Don't push them
  "Sometimes my mom asks me what's wrong, and she pushes me and pushes me, even if I say I don't want to talk about it. It's obvious that she cares for me, but sometimes boundaries aren't respected. She has the best intentions, but sometimes the way she shows them isn't the best way."
  —Kelly, thirteen, New Jersey

- ### Just sit with them
  "My mom understands that there are all these new emotions you feel when you're going through puberty. If I'm crying, she'll be totally understanding if I don't want to talk about it—she'll just sit down next to me and stroke my hair. When someone asks, 'What happened?!' it makes you cry harder because you're embarrassed."
  —Ali, thirteen, Florida

Girls Talk: Their Ideal Relationship with Their Parents

"I still need some responsibility, but I'd like them to get things more from my point of view too. That they wouldn't freak out or judge me."

—Kalli, eleven, Florida

"That I could trust them, but they'd understand that I have my privacy."

—Jessie, thirteen, Georgia

"To be able to talk with them without worrying that they'll get upset with me. To be closer, and feel like they're on my side."

—Elena, thirteen, Washington

"If we were able to spend more time just talking about how things are. Making more jokes, laughing more, having a sit-down dinner. That'd be the ideal."

—Hayley, twelve, Washington

What else is there to help parents and tweens communicate and get along better? You guessed it: the three takeaways to downplay the drama are just as important for dealing with family issues as they are for tackling the drama at school.

Her anchor activity will help her take her mind off whatever might be tense at home and will help her channel that energy into something positive. And if it's an activity in which the adults in her life can participate in some way—watching her perform in the orchestra or kick the winning goal at a soccer tournament—then it can be a bonding moment for you both. Looking up and seeing that you're in the stands or audience, proudly supporting her, goes a long way toward healing whatever wounds your disagreements might cause. Her helping hand can be a way to connect too. Parents and adults can join in their tween girl's service project. It's an easy way to spend positive time together. But an older mentor might be the most important of the takeaways when it comes to improving communication with your tween.

As you know, Christie was a godsend. And just like my grandfather and Parks were strong male supporters, I was also gifted with two older female mentors—my English teacher, Ms. Presley, and my middle school librarian, Mrs. Lentz. I could talk to them without being judged, and if they did worry about me, it wasn't on a parental level. I didn't need someone to hold me as I cried—my parents did that most of the time—I needed someone to say to me, "You can do it!"

They helped in different ways. Mrs. Lentz listened and sympathized. Ms. Presley related to a lot of what I was going through; by sharing her personal experiences as a middle schooler and high schooler, she made me feel normal and validated. Talking to both women helped me with my family relationships too; I didn't feel like I needed to carry as much sadness home.

"I tell my older cousin literally everything. It helps a lot because she's been through a lot, and she'll tell me things and

give me advice. Without her, it would be way different—I'd have a lot more stress and my problems would bother me more."

—Jessie, thirteen, Georgia

"My friend who's in high school has always been a positive influence. We became close through our car pool. She's been teaching me what it's like in high school and how it's going to be. I already know that your lockers are going to stick and you're going to be late for all your classes."

—Valerie, twelve, Michigan

High Schoolers Decode: We See That We Help as Adopted Older Sisters

"I see that the girls really look up to us and want to listen to us. We teach lessons similar to what their parents teach, but they want to listen to us because we're high schoolers. I think they want to hear what we have to say. I hope they apply it to their lives."

—Brooke, fourteen

"I think sharing in our Girl Talk meetings made things easier at home, especially with girls who had bad relationships with parents. Just to know that good relationships are possible is enough to try to improve their relationships."

—Grace, eighteen

A mentor is the absolute best gift you can give your middle school girl. I've seen it over and over in my own life and the lives of those around me. Without a doubt, giving her a positive high school female role model, someone to look up to and relate to, is the single most effective way to help a middle school girl. It not only helps your daughter but it helps you, too: the high schooler acts as a bridge between the two of you.

As I mentioned in Chapter 5, you can take an active role in seeking out your daughter's mentor. In fact, the relationship works best that way, because her adopted older sister is someone you trust, not just any high schooler your daughter thinks is cool. Your middle schooler doesn't even need to know that you have a relationship with her mentor; you can just tell the older girl, "Just let me know if anything comes up that I need to know about, but otherwise, I want her to feel comfortable coming to you."

Maybe it's the babysitter your daughter loved or a neighbor, but you can also ask the guidance counselor at the local high school if he or she can think of any older girls who might be a great adopted older sister for your daughter. "I think you're a great role model, and I know you won't steer her wrong," you can say. You can even formalize it and treat it as an after-school job, almost like babysitting: "On Tuesdays and Thursdays, I'd love to pay you for X hours— pick her up, help her with her homework, and end with ice cream." Everyone is winning here, because the high schooler will be proud to be a role model and see that she can make a difference in someone's life.

When I was in high school, I had this kind of relationship with an amazing middle school girl, Brooke. I had started Girl Talk and had taken a stand against the mean girl cycle, and her mother, Lisa, figured I could relate to her daughter.

High Schoolers Look Back: Our Mentors Helped Us

"I had a couple of teachers who I'd vent to. Having someone who's not a parent reassures girls that someone gets what they're going through. They're not there to judge you or critique your decisions. It actually improves your relationships at home because you're not bringing home what's bothering you at school."

—Alyssa, sixteen

"I had a really good family friend who's four years older than me. She'd just gone through the same stuff, and was always a good role model: good grades, really put together, her parents are friends with my parents so they were similar in discipline. She taught me a lot and made me a lot more mature—she'd tell me things I felt were a big deal weren't a big deal, and I realized I needed to be more mature about it and think about it more realistically."

—Fiona, sixteen

"I went to my older neighbor. She's so fun to be around, and my sister and I really felt like we could go to her for anything, especially when my parents were getting divorced. She was really good at getting our mind off of things. We'd be watching TV, and she'd ask, 'How's your mom and dad?' She didn't pry; she was just interested and available."

—Britney, sixteen

Though the two had a close relationship, Lisa could see the benefits of having someone else for Brooke to talk to. She came to me and said exactly what I've suggested above: "Could you bring her home from school once a week, maybe stop by TCBY, help her with her homework, and keep an eye out for her in the hallway?" I was so flattered that she'd asked, and I loved it. Soon, Brooke became an adopted younger sister, and Lisa became a confidant for me as I was going through high school. I'd encourage Brooke, taking her to movies or to get a pedicure, and Lisa and I would talk about the program I was starting, and school and guys—so she supported *me* too.

Meeting one day a week soon became two days a week, and eventually I told Lisa I couldn't be paid for it—they were like family by that point. It became apparent that we had started a really cool cycle: because of our relationship, when Brooke entered high school, she became a Girl Talk Leader, mentoring younger girls—just as I'd mentored her.

Next, we'll get into the details of what often makes home life hard during these years: those ongoing arguments and disagreements over boundaries and limits, rules and responsibilities.

Try This:
Help Her Get Along with You

- **Make a compromise list.** When an argument starts between you and your middle school girl, put this process in place: Each of you writes three compromises to whatever caused the argument. Compare your compromises until you reach a fair agreement.

- **Ask her to write down her solution.** When your tween girl doesn't agree with your handling of a situation or giving a certain punishment, ask her to write down what she thinks is the right way to handle the situation. You'll understand where your tween is coming from and maybe you'll both understand each other better.

The Bottom Line

- It's completely natural for girls to share less with their parents as they go through middle school.

- Often girls are extremely worried that parents and adults will judge them or change their perceptions of the tween, or that they'll experience repercussions for opening up.

- Gain her trust by making time for her, listening to her, letting her experiment with her identity, keeping her secrets, sharing more of your own experiences and stories, and making sure you're speaking to her in a loving way.

- While all three takeaways can help girls deal with their relationship with their parents, having an adopted older sister is key, since the adopted older sister can act as a trusted guide when the tween is no longer sharing as much with the positive adults in her life.

CHAPTER EIGHT

It's Not Fair!

Boundaries and Consequences

"My parents' opinions change so fast. If I could choose a theme song for them, it'd be that Katy Perry 'Hot N Cold' song: 'It's yes then it's no.' They're all over the place. . . . I understand she's my mom and has the right to control my life, but sometimes I want a spaceship to pick her up and zoom her to Mars."

—Bridget, thirteen, New Jersey

I don't want to speak for my parents and siblings, but I think it's safe to say that we all made each other crazy during my middle school years. We didn't deal with huge issues, but the day-to-day clashes at home really took their toll. We had one family computer for five people, so we bickered about who was allowed to be on it and for how long. I always wanted to sleep until the last possible minute each morning, often skipping breakfast, which infuriated my mom. And my parents wouldn't let me have a phone, computer, or TV in my room, even though I thought I was definitely old enough for those things. Plus, it made me crazy when it seemed like my sister and brother were getting away with things that I would've gotten in trouble for when I was their age. The list goes on and on. This all added up to a general atmosphere of arguing. We didn't have huge days-long fights, but these little things were ongoing, making us all feel at one point or another that we had to get out of the house before we went crazy.

So I wasn't surprised when I asked our community of middle school girls and parents what causes the most fights in their house and found similar responses. Overwhelmingly these girls mentioned boundaries, rules, and consequences: what they're allowed to do, what they're not allowed to do, what rules they considered unfair, and so on.

These fights can encompass anything from low-level bickering to all-out battles at the dinner table. And they're classic—they're the same arguments parents and kids have had for a long time. Your middle school girl wants independence, but she also wants to feel safe and protected. Often she's asking for more freedom than you're willing to give, and you might not be sure what to give her anyway since she's at this in-between stage. Some days it seems as if you're dealing with a mature young woman, and other days, it feels as if she's a little kid. But the more you're mentally prepared for these things—the more you realize that it'll be a roller coaster—the less surprising it'll be.

At the same time, the brave new world of technology has been added to the mix. Where are the rules when it comes to cell phones and texting, social networking and computer privileges? Where are the lines? What's too strict? Not strict enough? And is there anything you can say besides, "Because I'm the parent" or "Well, life's not fair"? (You'll hear more about this later, but girls tell me they'd love to compromise more.)

If you're feeling frustrated by not knowing where to draw the line with your middle schooler, you're not alone. Here's what Rachel, a middle school mom, has to say about her daughter: "She has an attitude, and sometimes I wonder if I'm handling it correctly. If I ask her to do something around the house, there's always a look, like, 'I can't believe you're asking me to do this. I *always* have to fold clothes!'" Mallory, another middle school mom, is frustrated by what she perceives as her daughter's lack of empathy: "Leaving the dirty dishes means someone else has to do them; being late means now I'm late to my thing. A lot of times we're fighting about things she doesn't think are important because she doesn't realize how it affects other people."

But even when she argues with you, chances are that your middle schooler realizes where you're coming from—to some extent. From my conversations with girls, I've found that they usually understand that rules and boundaries are there to protect them. Most of the time, they said, their parents' rules and punishments made sense. "My parents are pretty fair, although they're often overprotective," says Hayley, a Washington seventh grader. "Sometimes I wish that they wouldn't be, but there are some things I didn't end up doing because they told me I couldn't, and at the time I was mad, but I might've ended up hurt if I had."

Your style of disciplining your kids is affected by countless factors. Each child poses her own unique challenges and calls for different parenting styles.

My parents dealt with my siblings and me in separate ways. I created huge expectations for myself academically, and I had an innate fear of disappointing people, so my parents didn't really need to set boundaries for me around curfews, bedtimes, or my responsibilities around the house—I set them for myself. My sister was the complete opposite.

Girls Talk: What Causes the Most Tension between Tweens and Their Parents

- Grades: not achieving as parents expect
- Schoolwork: doing other activities instead of studying
- Home chores: who's responsible for what task
- Freedom among friends: differing parental rules within groups of friends

"She's too hard on me. I'm grounded for a B. I got grounded for getting an A, just because I forgot two pieces of homework. I hate how hard she drives homework. I'm already known as the nerd in school; I don't want to also be known as the nerd who does nothing else but study."

—Kalli, eleven, Florida

"Everything. I could just want some water, and I could ask her to get it, and if I've asked for a favor previously, we'll start fighting about that. Small little things set each of us off, and we get annoyed—and finally one of us will just snap."

—Sam, twelve, Washington

She's more of a free spirit, the don't-fence-me-in type, so when she was younger, she needed specific bedtimes and rules. My brother needed TV limits to prevent him from spending all of his time flipping channels. Though I didn't care about TV, I would've stayed online and on Instant Messenger for hours if my parents didn't control it.

Oldest children have a unique set of challenges. Since they're the ones paving the way, the oldest may often feel that their younger siblings are given more privileges than they were allowed at the same age. That can be a source of frustration to the oldest and a relief to the younger siblings, as sixteen-year-old Girl Talk Leader Alyssa says: "I had an older sister, so my parents had been through it once—the makeup and cell phones. But if you're the oldest sibling, then you have to fight all those battles, and that can make it more difficult."

And whether it's conscious or subconscious, girls are also expected to please others, and they feel pressure to be perfectly smart, perfectly sweet, and perfectly athletic. For girls, it can sometimes feel like a no-win situation: no matter how hard they try, no matter how much pressure they're under from all sides, it can feel that their parents still assume they could easily fall off track. Many girls expressed something along these lines, although not always explicitly; they wonder why, even if they try to do everything right and they've never been in major trouble, their parents won't let them do X, Y, or Z. "On some level, they trust me to not do anything stupid, like drugs," says thirteen-year-old Bridget in New Jersey. "But when they start asking questions like, 'Are you sure?' 'Are you lying?' Then it makes me upset, like, *Wow they don't trust me. I can't believe he doesn't trust that I'm not going to go against his rules.*"

A few other themes emerged in our conversations with girls—things that parents may not consciously realize are affecting their arguments about rules and boundaries. Here's what girls said they'd like parents to keep in mind when they're setting boundaries and punishing them for breaking rules.

What Parents Don't Realize

How much a tween's social life is affected when she isn't allowed to do something.

Of course your middle schooler's safety will trump her always-shifting spot in the social hierarchy. It probably doesn't matter to you if she's the only one not going to a party. But when there's so much social pressure, it makes sense that girls say their parents don't understand how frustrating it can be when their friends are allowed to do something and they're not. Parents have heard this time and time again: "But so-and-so can go!"

To girls, though, it's not a whining excuse since it feels very real. When everyone else is at the dance on Friday night and she's in her room because her parents won't let her go, or when everyone was invited to a party through Facebook and since she didn't have an account, she missed the invitation—you know what? It's miserable for her. And all she can do is think about all the fun she's missing out on. Often girls honestly don't understand why their parents have said no when other parents have said yes. (It's one of the reasons that girls have told us that the more their parents explain the reasoning behind their rules, the more accepting and less angry they are about them.) "The rule has been that I can't text or talk to guys over the phone, and that seems so weird," says Kaitlin, a thirteen-year-old in Georgia. "At school I can still talk to guys, and over the weekends I talk to guys during my basketball games; my friends text guys all the time, and their parents are fine with it. It feels really weird that my friends are taking part in something that I can't. I feel left out."

It seems especially unjustified if she feels like she's a "good" girl who always follows the rules, like thirteen-year-old Kelly in New Jersey. "I'll be on the phone like, 'I gotta

High Schoolers Look Back: We Dealt with It Too

"Most of my friends had cell phones in middle school, and I couldn't get one until I could drive. I begged and begged. It made me really angry; I always felt like she was impeding my social life. I don't think my mom realized that I was so upset because it made me different from the other kids."

—Ashley, eighteen

"When I went to school, everyone would've been talking on text or Facebook, and I'd get to class and not know what was going on."

—Heidi, fourteen

go, I can't talk to you.' My friends will say, 'Can't you stay up for five more minutes?' It's so frustrating, like, why are they so strict? I get to school on time; I get all my homework done. Why can't I stay up for ten more minutes?"

Another thing girls thought parents didn't realize:

It's confusing when rules are enforced without consistency or explanation and when the punishment doesn't seem to fit the crime.

Any number of things can lead parents to be inconsistent: different situations demand different responses; your own life circumstances affect your mood. Girls often don't understand that their parents *are* only human, after all.

But considering that middle school is such an unstable time for girls, it's only natural that they crave consistency during these few years. The trust issues that have come up repeatedly throughout—wondering whom they can really trust when it seems that everything around them is constantly changing—are very much at play here.

You can do a lot to help your tween feel that her world is stable, and to help her trust you more by being as consistent as you can and offering as much explanation as possible for the reasons behind your decisions. Here's Kelly, the New Jersey eighth grader, on the inconsistencies she sees in her parents' discipline: "Sometimes my parents will check the time of my last text, and if they catch me texting after bedtime, they'll take away my phone for two weeks. I don't get it: they'll let me stay up late if I have to finish my homework assignment, but one text and the phone is gone?"

Without consistency, parents' rules can seem arbitrary, created and enforced on a whim. Kaitlin, a Georgia thirteen-year-old, also feels confused by what she sees as her mother's random disciplinary action. "Sometimes I've talked back to her, and she yells at me and makes me feel bad about myself, but there's no actual punishment," says Kaitlin. "Later I'll want to do something, and she doesn't want me to do it, and then she reminds me that I talked back to her. By the time I get the consequences, the action was a month ago and I thought we'd moved on, but she pulls it back and makes me feel bad again."

What Are Normal Boundaries and Rules?

Everyone parents differently and has their own sets of rules, so what's right for one household might not work in another. It's important to be encouraging and respectful of other parents' rules and boundaries even if you don't agree with them. "We're doing what feels right to us, given our experiences and the kind of environment we'd like in our home," says Susan, a middle school mom. "But we have dear friends whose rules and boundaries are quite different for children of the same age—and we have no reason to suspect that their children will have any major issues as a result."

Just as girls often ask me what's "normal" in terms of what they're going through at school and home, parents often ask me the same thing about discipline. They're interested in what other parents are doing. So I asked our far-reaching community of middle schoolers, high schoolers, and parents to define their boundaries—things like curfews, chores, and limits on using technology. This information can be used as a conversational starting point for you and your tween.

When you were a middle schooler and dealing with your own parents, you probably faced some of these same issues, like curfews and home responsibilities. Even with all the generational differences, your parents and even grandparents probably dealt with similar topics and certain expectations. But with the prevalence of technology, today's parents are forging rules and boundaries in a completely new world. You can't look back to what frustrated you about how your family handled texting, or ask your parents for advice on how many hours they let you stay online, or whether they allowed adults to "friend" you on Facebook. These online spaces didn't exist before. (No wonder disagreements about social networking and texting seem to make up the bulk of family arguments about boundaries today.) We're still establishing norms for this ever-changing world of technology. It'll continue to be trial and error, especially as girls' expectations transform alongside these new technologies.

Susan, a middle school mom, says that limiting her kids' use of technology early on worked for her family. "It's very hard to build a fence where people are already standing," she says. "It's much easier to know your boundaries in advance, and manage activities so you're never likely to actually reach them. We didn't want video games or TV to become a need for our kids, so we didn't allow video games for many years and limited TV time from the start, so that they were forced to develop other interests—which they did. We did the same with the computer and phones: limiting their use early forced them to get into the habit of spending their time on other activities."

Here's what our community of girls, high schoolers, and parents had to say about everyday boundaries:

What's a fair curfew for a middle schooler?

Most girls and high schoolers said: Weeknights: 9:00 to 10:00 P.M., weekends: 10:30 P.M. to midnight.

> *"On a weeknight, a fair curfew is 9:30. As I get older, it gets higher."*
>
> —Tera, eleven, California

Should she be expected to do homework right after school—or should parents give her some breathing room?

Most girls said: Actually, they'd *rather* do it right after school—but they'd like thirty minutes of space first.

> *"I come home, eat a snack, do my homework, and I'm happy I've gotten it over with."*
>
> —Kaitlin, thirteen, Georgia

> *"Having a half-hour to eat a snack and chill for a while is good."*
>
> —Tabitha, eleven, New York

What home responsibilities are fair?

Most girls said: Keeping bedroom clean, helping out to make dinner or to do dishes afterward, feeding pets, doing own laundry.

High Schoolers Look Back: Chore Wars

I learned to just do it

"In middle school, I definitely complained about my chores a lot more. By high school I realized that even if I complained, I'd still have to do them, and it would just take a lot more time. Now I just get them done: I know it's the rule, and it's not going to change."

—Imani, sixteen

My mom used chores against us

"My mom took out her anger and frustration on my sister and me through our chores. She'd make us clean the house on Friday nights instead of letting us go to a friend's house. Or we'd be planning to go out, and at the last minute she'd say, 'Oh no, I have something for you to do'—and it would be cleaning."

—Britney, sixteen

How much (nonhomework) computer and TV time is okay each day?

Most girls and parents said: The computer: thirty minutes to two hours. TV: Not really an issue, since TV is now available online and can be recorded and watched over the weekend.

> *"I can have both my computer and TV on, as long as I've done my homework and my grades are up."*
> —Max, thirteen, Florida

> *"I'm afraid that my mom will monitor what I do on the computer. I don't do anything wrong, like talk to strangers. But my mom might not approve of some of the stuff that me and my friends joke about. My computer is my social and personal life; it's important to me that it's mine."*
> —Kalli, eleven, Florida

When should cell phones be turned off? When should texting be off-limits?

Girls and parents said the same thing: Overnight, at school, during family dinners, at religious services, during homework and studying, at the movies.

> *"Our kids know that the phone is a convenience for us, not them. If we text or call them, they need to answer quickly. If we can't get in touch with them, they'll lose their phones and more, depending on the situation."*
> —Jennifer, middle school mom

Should parents see what they text?

Girls overwhelmingly said: No.

> *"Parents don't trust you if they're looking at your texts. I really don't think it's fair to go through the kids' texts and*

What Parents Say about Texting

Don't text and talk
"Our rule is that if you are face-to-face with someone, you give that person your attention and put the phone aside. It's the same thing when we're together as a family, even on a long car ride: that's the time to engage directly."

—Susan, middle school mom

It can be a secret bond between parents and kids
"If they're at a party and are ready to leave but don't want to make a big deal out of it, they can send a text and not draw attention to themselves. It's important when a situation comes up that they could be uncomfortable with."

—Jennifer, middle school mom

"It's easy for them and not embarrassing. No one knows they're talking with their parents."

—Lori, middle school mom

ask questions. Occasionally they ask who I'm texting, but I mostly only text four or five girls."

—Kaitlin, thirteen, Georgia

"Not unless you're disobeying the texting rule. It's a private conversation. It'd be like eavesdropping on a normal conversation with your friend."

—Courtney, twelve, New Jersey

When is it okay to have a Facebook or social networking site? Should parents be able to see what they post?

High schoolers, parents (and Facebook itself) all say: When a girl is thirteen.

Most girls say: Thirteen as well, but most have rules to friend a parent.

"About once a month my parents look at my Facebook wall, and they're like, 'Okay, that's cool.' It doesn't bother me that they look at it: I talk to my friends on Facebook like I would if I was standing right beside my parents."

—Kaitlin, thirteen, Georgia

"They used to be really embarrassing. It's like, I know you love me, you don't have to write it all over my Facebook wall."

—Kelly, thirteen, New Jersey

Should teachers, coaches, and other nonfamily adults be allowed to friend middle schoolers?

Most parents said: No.

"Teachers should maintain a professional boundary. I tell them that we can be friends on Facebook when they graduate from high school or college. By then, they don't care.

Parents Talk: Our Facebook Rules

"My daughter signed a media agreement with me on the use of her cell phone, e-mail, and Facebook account. We said, 'You may not mention anything about this family, our work, or specify any location.' And we'd have to approve any photos she posted."

—Jane, middle school mom

"Our rules are: they have to give us their password, they have to friend us, we have to be able to view their wall, and all posts must be positive or neutral—no negative posts about people. My daughter posted something like, 'Teachers are mean,' and I made her delete the post and took away Facebook for two weeks."

—Jennifer, middle school mom

And if a student friended me, I would explain why I don't and ignore the request."

—Peyton, middle school teacher

Should parents of your tween's friends be allowed to friend middle schoolers? (Could it help your tween be even more accountable for what she posts if she knows her friends' parents are reading her updates, too?)

Most parents said: Depends on who the adult is and how they're communicating with the tween (casual chatting isn't okay, but congratulating her on a great basketball game might be).

"I actually like to be 'friends' with the kids: it allows me a window into their real world and lets me know their true character."

—Julie, middle school mom

Of course, this isn't to say that technology is only a scary world, full of dangers for your middle schooler. Our high school girls talk about the great things that come from spending more time online beyond the normal e-mailing and online research—things like being able to more easily figure out their finances and pay cell phone bills. And parents see the benefits too. "Using e-mail as much as they do will prepare them for the real world," says Jennifer, a middle school mom. "My children have heard from the beginning that if you can't stand in front of 500 people and tell

225

the truth, then it's not worth saying. Or if you can't print it on the front page of the newspaper, don't send it in an e-mail, text, or Facebook post."

Parents Talk:
Facebook Fears

"I'm really afraid of some nasty clique devastating my daughter and calling it out on Facebook. Or that they'd make some stupid video and it gets out on the Web. Technology has brought some wonderful great things, but also a whole different level of fear for parents."

—Mallory, middle school mom

"I think it becomes a tremendous time sink for kids who could be doing so many other productive things. And it's an easy way to increase the drama by giving young girls another avenue to say hurtful things, which they might never have the gumption to say directly."

—Susan, middle school mom

"Social media creates a second social life on top of an already busy real time social life. It's as if the kids never get a break from the pressure."

—Jennifer, middle school mom

Just-Been-There Advice:
What Pictures Are Okay on Facebook?

"Anything but pictures that you wouldn't want to be on CNN if you run for a Senate seat."

—Annie, eighteen

"Pictures of kissing a boy, drinking, smoking, and wearing too little clothing—that's all inappropriate. But pictures of travel, sports, friends, and family are all okay."

—Carey, fifteen

"Don't post pictures that reveal where you live, or that hurt other friends' feelings if they weren't invited. If it's a picture of anyone else, you should ask your friends for permission first."

—Haven, sixteen

"Pictures that you wouldn't mind your grandmother or teachers seeing."

—Imani, sixteen

How can you promote more peace around the house? Most of our high schoolers say that compromising is the key. Not only will it help to end the arguments, but it gives tweens the feeling that they're being heard and respected, say our teen mentors. "My dad made it really clear that I couldn't have a boyfriend until I was sixteen, but in eighth grade, a boy asked me out," recalls Grace, eighteen. "We compromised that I couldn't go on a date to the movies by myself, but I could go if there were a lot of other people with us. We did the same thing in seventh grade when I wanted to start going to the mall by myself—the compromise was that my mom had to be in the mall, but I could walk around with a friend without her."

Fiona's family compromised by setting up "trades." "If I helped my younger sister do something, then they'd let me do something I wasn't normally allowed to do," says the sixteen-year-old. "Or if I talked back to them and then I wanted to go somewhere, they'd say, 'Well, you talked back to us.' I'd say, 'What can I do to make up for it?'"

Whether you compromise or not, you might feel as if you're *always* arguing about homework or whether she can post a certain photo on Facebook, or when texting is okay. Girls do want freedom, but they also want structure and accountability; you're probably not too far from the time your girl will look back and understand your reasons for making the rules you made.

High Schoolers Look Back: We Get It Now

"I would've liked to have friends over and gone over to their houses more often. When you can't drive yourself, it's about whether your parents can get you around, and they both worked long hours—nothing they could've changed.

I understand now, but at the time it's like, 'You don't want me to have fun!'"

—Annie, eighteen

"My friends were allowed to go to concerts, and the movies, and the mall before me. It was embarrassing, and I thought it was about trust; I was upset that they didn't trust me. But now I realize they were just scared, since I'm the oldest. It wasn't about trusting me but trusting the people around me."

—Fiona, sixteen

"In one of our recent Girl Talk meetings, a girl didn't understand why her mom wouldn't let her go to the movies with a guy. It helps that I know what they're going through and why they're upset. I said, 'That's because she doesn't want you to get hurt; she's doing it with good reason to protect you.'"

—Imani, sixteen

As we discussed in the last chapter, the three takeaways to downplay the drama can help your girl deal with frustrations at home. An anchor activity allows her to temporarily put aside the arguments at home and immerse herself in something positive, and the helping hand is a reminder that her issues with your rules and boundaries can be pretty small compared to the serious problems facing some people in her community. And her adopted older sister will give her both a safe place to vent and an understanding that bickering over rules is a normal stage—one that will change as she gets older.

Next, we'll look at what happens when the drama at home isn't just about rules and limits—when your tween is struggling with much larger and more serious issues.

Try This: Help Her Understand Your Boundaries

- **Offer a reward.** Together decorate a jar or box that you can use to reward her good behavior, good grades, and good decisions. For every ten things you add to the jar, she's allowed a boundary reward, like staying out an hour later on the weekends or having a friend sleep over during the school week. This can be a great way to build trust between you and your middle school girl.
- **Sign a media contract.** Ask your tween to draft a media contract that she thinks is fair and reasonable. Have her include things like time spent on Facebook, what photos she can upload, and who she can video-chat with, for example. Review it with her and make the necessary compromises. Let her know that as she gets older and more responsible, you're open to discussing and modifying the contract.

The Bottom Line

- Girls say that the most frequent arguments at home are about boundaries and rules. Each tween might call for a different set of rules and limits, but girls say that consistency is important in helping them understand and respect your rules.

- Girls want parents to take into account how their social life might be affected by their parents' limitations. They'd also like parents to make sure that their discipline fits the crime.

- Ultimately girls understand why rules are set, but explaining your reasoning will help her trust you, which will help her feel heard and respected.

- Showing your tween that you're willing to compromise will go a long way toward building mutual trust and respect.

CHAPTER NINE

Getting Serious

When the Drama Is Very Real

"I have a friend with a perfect family: they eat together every night and talk to each other about everything. They have awesome conversations. I'm jealous of that. I always wish I had that."

—Charlotte, twelve, California

"I feel like there's a lot that's unsaid, that's just sitting in between the lines of our family. I feel like there's this huge gap of secrets. And I don't know what that is."

—Hayley, twelve, Washington

One evening during sixth grade, I went over to my friend Lauren's house for a sleepover. I'd known Lauren since we were born; I'd been over to her house lots of times, and I knew her family well. So I was completely taken aback that night when she started to cry. "My parents are splitting up," she confided. "I have no idea who I'm going to live with or who's moving out." She seemed heartbroken and in shock—she loved them both so much. It was as if someone had taken her life and turned it completely upside down, shaking her sense of stability and safety.

My mom asked if I'd had fun when she picked me up the next morning, and I started crying as I told her Lauren's news. Mom hugged me and revealed that she had already known what happened, but wanted me to hear it from Lauren directly. She didn't want Lauren to think anyone had been gossiping about her family. "It gives you a chance to be a good friend," she said. "What she needs is someone to be there for her. She's going to need you, and I wanted her to have the chance to lean on you."

For weeks after, I was haunted by Lauren's revelation. What if the same thing happened to my parents? I'd dealt with friend drama and worried about Mom's eye disease and our financial situation—but this was the first big family situation I had encountered. It was the first time I realized that life can change in an instant, no matter how certain you think it is.

Lauren seemed to shut down after that. Now that I look back on it, I think she just wasn't equipped to handle the situation (Who really is?). She was angry and distant. She got in arguments with her friends, and her grades dropped; the divorce touched every aspect of her life. From our conversations over the next few years, it seemed that Lauren's main source of frustration was the feeling that she could no longer trust her home life. She wanted to come home to a place that felt safe and protected, but instead she worried about her lack of stability both at school and home.

Family problems can hit girls hard during these middle school years. This isn't just a period of hormonal, social, emotional, and psychological changes; it's also the time when girls become much more aware of the dynamics of their families. It might seem as if your daughter is completely wrapped up in her own life (and that's likely true), but by middle school, she's present enough to know about things that might be happening under the surface at home, like divorce, health problems, fighting, financial crises—all the big family troubles that can hit when least expected.

It's easier to protect children from these harsh realities in elementary school; their age renders them somewhat oblivious and quick to rebound. And by high school, they seem mature enough to handle some of it on their own. Greater independence with friends, maybe a first big relationship, the ability to drive and have a part-time job: these can all serve to help a high schooler manage the stress of whatever might be going on at home.

But middle schoolers are literally stuck in the middle. Not only is this likely the time for girls to become aware of something happening at home that they might have been protected from before—parents divorcing, a sibling battling an illness—but there often isn't a way for middle schoolers to channel that stress and sadness. And as families' schedules get even busier with less time for serious talking, parents can sometimes feel lost as to what their daughter is struggling with, as Mallory, a parent of a sixth grader, found:

"Her father and I are divorced, and it seems fine—but what happens if later on she has really messed-up relationship issues? It's the things I can't see coming that worry me. I won't know if she has commitment issues; I don't know how to look for the hidden things. At least if I know about it, I can figure out the solution—but it's the not knowing. You're so used to knowing everything about your child, and when

you release them to middle school, there are a lot of interac-
tions you're not a part of. If there was a serious weight issue
or drug issue, or something terrible happened to her—those
are the ones kids don't recover from and become screwed-
up adults. You can handle it with therapy, but that's some
serious core damage."

Most of the girls interviewed for *The Drama Years* hadn't experienced major life trauma. But for those that had, it typically fell into one of two camps: big family problems like divorce, and depression and self-harm. Since these are the issues that seemed most prevalent, these are the ones I'll discuss here. Even if your girl isn't dealing with these problems, maybe they're affecting a friend or a family member.

Of course, there are lots of other problems they might be tackling—eating disorders, abuse, and underage drinking are just a few of them. Check out the Resources section at the back of this book for a list of Web sites, organizations, and books that cover these serious topics.

Dealing with Family Trauma

Take all of the changes we've talked about in this book, add on some major family issue—without the coddling your kids will get in elementary school or the freedom to escape that they'll have in high school—and you'll see why this is one of the hardest times for kids to deal with something traumatic at home. No wonder the girls who'd dealt with family trouble talked about experiencing a general feeling of mistrust: what they'd come to rely on as real, like their parents' relationship, wasn't what it seemed. "Recently, during a fight, my mom said, 'I don't love your father anymore,'" says Hayley, a seventh grader in Washington. "And now I'm looking at my life in all sorts of different ways. The times we've all spent together as a family. Was that a lie?"

Charlotte, a twelve-year-old Californian, echoes that feeling of not being able to trust her parents. "Their divorce was a long time ago, but there's still a lot of fighting," she says. "I hear two different sides of the story. If I ask one parent, 'Why did you get divorced?' they say totally different things. So I don't really trust either of them. One of them has to be lying, and I don't know who."

Bridget, a New Jersey eighth grader, points to the impact of her family's instability: her feelings of being overwhelmed and not being able to do well in school. "Some part of me doesn't want to believe what happened, that my dad cheated on my mom, but I know it's true," she says. "You don't want to think that your parents would do something so stupid. It all makes it really hard to focus on school. You don't want to fail, but the whole time it's like, 'Why is this so sudden?' 'Why is this happening?' It's just sad. It's a lot to take in at once."

Of course, not every family has major issues. Many of our girls talked not about their own stories but those of their friends—and their confusion of not knowing how to help a friend who's dealing with something major, as Elena and Jessie say:

"A good friend of mine stopped coming to school. Recently my mom found out that she was struggling with depression and on medication. I had no idea; I was so shocked. I guess she felt like she had no friends. I thought, 'What if this was partly my fault? What if I wasn't as good of a friend to

her as I meant to be?' I don't know how to deal with that.
I don't know if people want sympathy, like, 'Oh, you'll be
okay,' or if they just want me there. I don't want to say too
little and have them think I don't care, or to be overdra-
matic and overreact."

—Elena, thirteen, Washington

"You don't know what to say to your friends. You're walking
on ice because you don't know if you're going to say some-
thing bad that's going to upset them; you're not really sure."

—Jessie, thirteen, Georgia

Both girls want to reach out to their friends, but the fear
that they might say or do the wrong thing holds them back.
There are ways for these girls to be there for each other.

High Schoolers Look Back:
We Dealt with It Too

I felt like I was the only one
"My parent's divorce during seventh grade definitely
affected middle school. My sister and I knew my parents
had been fighting, but we didn't know it was that bad, so
it sort of hit us out of the blue; it was totally unexpected.
Not many people were open about their parents getting
divorced, so I felt very alone. I didn't really feel like I had
anyone to really go to, and that made it really hard."

—Britney, sixteen

I felt like they forgot about me in the midst of their problems

"Money was really tight in middle school, and my parents almost got divorced when I was in seventh grade. My mom packed her bags and left; she came back, but it was still hard. I had my own life too, and it felt like nothing that was going on in my life really mattered. I didn't have anywhere to turn for help. I stayed in my room all the time; I guess that was my way of dealing with it. I didn't know what else to do; every time I tried to talk to my parents about anything, they'd bring up that our problems were bigger than what I wanted to talk about. I wish I'd been able to talk to them more openly instead of keeping it all bottled up, because it comes out in a bad way eventually."

—Ashley, eighteen

Instability led me to feel disconnected from people my age

"My mother's an alcoholic and always has been, and my adopted father died from cirrhosis of the liver, so I've lived with my grandfather for as long as I can remember. I started to realize in fifth grade that something wasn't normal with my family. My mother would make plans to get me during the week to do something, and she'd never show up; I could never really trust her to do what she said she'd do. My grandfather did a good job of raising me, but he's two generations away, and it affected my relationships with other people, because I didn't know how to act around them. He didn't want me to talk to the other kids about why I didn't live with my parents. So I've always struggled to connect with other people. I've always been forced into a position where I was more mature than everyone around me. It made me look for that kind of relationship in other places, like a misplaced need for some kind of parent."

—Audrey, sixteen

How to Help Them Through

Since I'm not a therapist or psychologist, I can't give clinical advice or answers as to what's best for your middle schooler in the middle of a crisis or serious trauma. Every girl is different, and no situation is the same. For problems as big as these, professional help is key. But I *can* tell you what girls tell me.

For one, **they don't want to feel torn between their divorced parents.** It's easy for parents to forget that kids internalize what they hear, and when a parent is angry, it can be tough to rein in negative comments about their ex. But over and over, girls say that hearing gossip about one parent from the other is upsetting and uncomfortable, and it makes them angry and unsure how to respond. "They always want you to pick favorites; they're always competing to be the best parent," twelve-year-old Charlotte, from California, says. "They send hate e-mail to each other. They're like kids. And I feel like the messenger. They'll say, 'Tell the other parent this, this, and this,' and they put me in the middle. They blame everything on each other, and it's horrible." Eleven-year-old Tera, also from California, doesn't like being asked to choose between her mom and dad. "I want to do things with both of them, and they get in arguments about who should take me," she says. "Sometimes my dad will say, 'How about you come here?' and my mom will say the same thing. I know it means a lot to both of them, so I don't know which one to choose."

High Schoolers Look Back: We Were Caught in the Middle Too

"They'd use [my sister and me] to talk to each other. And if I talked to one of them about the other, it'd be like blackmail for the first parent: if I talked to Mom about Dad, my mom would say something to him. Plus, we'd feel bad if we did something with Dad, because we knew we were leaving our mom out— but we also know we couldn't do anything as the four of us, even though we wanted to."

—Britney, sixteen

Dealing with family problems when everyone they know seems to be part of a happy family unit can make girls feel even more alienated and alone than they might have been already. Eighteen-year-old Kendall recalls what middle school was like for her after her mother developed a brain tumor. "My friends couldn't understand," she says. "Everything was perfectly fine with their moms and dads. I hardly talked to them about what happened at home. They'd ask how she was doing and I'd put it aside. Sometimes I wished they were more concerned." This points to another way that parents can help girls through: Since girls often feel that they can't talk to friends their own age about family drama, it's even more important to **surround them with people they *can* talk to**—an adopted older sister, another mentor, a therapist, or another trusted adult.

A third thing that girls need parents to do is to **tell the truth about what's going on at home.** If you've chosen to keep something from your child, you obviously have a good reason—but girls often know more about what's going on than you might think. And if you're hiding something from them, they're less likely to trust you, says Heidi, a fourteen-year-old mentor. "The worst thing about my mother's depression was that no one told me what was really going on," she explains. "Things would've been better if they'd been more open and honest from the beginning. I would've had more of a connection with them, like, 'You tell me stuff and I'll be able to tell you stuff back.' I didn't trust them because I knew they weren't telling me things. They should've given me more information about what was going on—not full details, but just enough so I'd understand."

She doesn't need the entire story, just the basic facts. It's incredibly uncomfortable for a girl to feel that her family is hiding a huge secret or avoiding some painful truth. These tweens can handle reality more than parents might think. "If my parents had told us more about their divorce, it would've made us feel more included and we would've understood it more," says sixteen-year-old Britney. "We were just supposed to accept it without understanding their reasoning. I understand that parents don't want to share everything, but there's a way to negotiate that. If they share a little bit, their kids will feel like they can trust them more."

In a similar vein, if something major is happening at home, they don't want you to act like everything's okay and nothing's going on. And *they* don't want to feel pressured to act happy when things obviously *aren't* okay. If parents are avoiding the truth, girls can see right through it, says Hayley, twelve, from Washington. They'll often come to the conclusion that they can't talk to that parent about the issue: "When my mom stopped seeing a counselor, it made me feel like she wants to ignore the divorce—and like she's not available to talk about it," she says. "If she's not doing counseling, she's not making an effort, and that's disappointing. I try to talk about it with her, but she pushes away the subject."

Hiding the truth is just putting off the inevitable anyway, says Britney, a sixteen-year-old mentor. Sooner or later, you'll have to deal with it. "During the divorce, my family put on this face where we pretended that everything was the same," she says. "In some ways it helps get through the day-to-day, but in the long run it's worse, because all the feelings are piling up. When I would pretend like it was okay and nothing was bothering me, I'd eventually break down; I couldn't take it anymore."

Girls are expected to act like this more than guys are, Britney adds: "There's more pressure on girls to act like everything's okay, because girls are more worried about what people are going to think than guys. Girls need to be happy; that way, they won't stand out and get negative attention." Girls already feel so much pressure to be perfect that adding this unreasonable put-on-a-happy-face expectation is throwing fuel on the fire. Brooke, fourteen, agrees: "There's pressure to stay put together for girls, at least at school and in public. I definitely feel it. It can become unhealthy: you need to let it out, at least every once in a while; otherwise you became a ball of emotions and then you break."

High Schoolers Look Back:
The Pressure to Act Okay Can Be Detrimental

"For me, it was all about keeping up the facade that everything's okay. I never wanted to draw any negative attention to myself. If I tried to be the best thing ever, no one could ever imagine that I live with my grandpa and my mother's psycho. And since I was trying to make everything seem apple pie perfect, it bled over into other aspects of my life, like, I don't like to admit I'm having problems. Pressure to act like things are okay hardens you emotionally. Eventually you get done with lying about your life and you just accept it. Parents have to know they have to let their kids express their emotions and grief in a positive way, because if they don't, it's going to come out negatively, eventually. It would've been easier if more people were around to talk to, if there was more of an outlet talking about it."

—Audrey, sixteen

Besides family issues, some of our middle schoolers had also struggled with depression—either their own or that of a family member or friend. "I think girls are more susceptible to depression than guys," says New Jersey seventh grader Courtney. "Girls create more drama than guys and make everything seem worse than it is; they overreact, and that makes them more depressed." Statistics about tween depression are hard to come by, but we know that about 14 percent of teenagers experience it and that it opens them up to being more at risk for other issues, like drug and alcohol abuse.

"My mom was pretty convinced that I was depressed over the summer," says Hayley, a twelve-year-old in Washington. "It felt like an emptiness around me. You feel like there's a shade covering you that you can't break out of; part of you is taken over, and you don't even want to break out of it, because there's something inside of you that's taking over. You have to push yourself out of it."

More and more girls today report that their classmates and friends are turning their feelings inward—and are using cutting or other self-harm as a means of dealing with feelings of unhappiness, boredom, or depression. "I think cutting is one of the least-talked-about subjects in school," says thirteen-year-old Jessie in Georgia. "It's becoming a serious problem. I haven't heard of anyone being bulimic, but I know all of these people who currently cut themselves, and I don't think it's talked about enough."

The term *cutting* encompasses many different forms of self-injury, according to sociologists Patricia Adler and Peter Adler, authors of *The Tender Cut: Inside the Hidden World of Self-Injury*, from the actual cutting of one's skin using a razor, knife, or other sharp object to burning, scratching, hitting, or puncturing oneself. Adler and Adler report that as more young people have turned to self-injury over the past decade, it has changed from a psychological disorder to a subculture. (No studies focus solely on girls between the ages of eleven and thirteen, but experts estimate that in the United States, one in every two hundred girls between the ages of thirteen and nineteen cuts herself regularly.) Nineteen-year-old actress and musician Demi Lovato has been open about her struggle with self-injury, telling the

High Schoolers Look Back: When She Was Depressed, an Older Friend Helped

"The whole transition to high school was really hard on me. I was questioning everything, from school to friends. Where did I belong? Why is this so hard on me? My best friend started ignoring me, and I was thinking, 'Who am I going to hang out with? Who will be my new best friend?' I cried a lot, and stopped doing what I usually did, and didn't read books or listen to music or talk to my friends. It lasted for three months.

"Finally, I talked to one of my older girlfriends. She encouraged me, and told me that if I kept feeling that way, I should get help or go to a therapist. And since we're both religious, she suggested I read the Bible for advice about depression. I found a lot of verses that really hit me. I realized, 'Wow, all of these people went through so much worse than I did; I have such a great life and so much before me; I shouldn't take it for granted.' My parents never knew, and I didn't tell most of my friends either. So having this older friend was so important. She'd check up on me and send me texts, like, 'How are you feeling today? Can I bring you something?' I eventually got back to normal, and now I try to look for signs of depression in my friends."

—Brooke, fourteen

news program *20/20* that she cut "as a way of expressing my own shame, of myself, on my own body. I was matching the inside to the outside. And there were some times where my emotions were just so built up, I didn't know what to do. The only way that I could get instant gratification was through an immediate release on myself."

Courtney, a New Jersey seventh grader, was frightened when she found out that a friend cut herself. "One of my friends was depressed all the time because her parents were getting divorced, and she used to cut herself," she says. "One day I saw the cut on her wrist, and I asked what it was. It's scary because I was thinking, 'What if this happened to me?' I tried to hang out with her more, and only fill her mind with happy things, and text her every day how great she was."

Jessie describes hearing why a friend turned to self-harm. "I've known eight or more girls who cut," she says. "One of my friends had a breakdown one day, everything was going wrong, and she was like, 'Forget this,' and cut herself. She's smart, pretty, a cheerleader, scholar, has a fan club—you wouldn't think she would. If you're going through pain, why would you want to give yourself more pain? But it wasn't like trying to kill herself. I think for some people, it's a release; you wouldn't keep doing something if you didn't enjoy it in some way. It must be like a pain-pleasure thing, like they wanted it to hurt, they wanted to feel it."

Most girls who cut aren't suicidal, according to Adler and Adler. But it's not something to be taken lightly. It's a sign that your tween needs help expressing her emotions safely.

High Schoolers Decode: Being a Cutter

"I was dealing with a lot of family problems and stress and anxiety, and I felt very angry—like I'd been holding in my emotions for years. One day after school, I came home and cut my wrist. I knew I was taking my anger out on myself. Suicide never even crossed my mind; I wasn't trying to kill myself. I was trying to release anger. I wish I'd had someone to talk to besides my parents. If I'd been able to express that all sooner, it could've come out in a healthier way."

—Ashley, eighteen

How to Help Them Through

If you have any concerns that your middle schooler could be dealing with these issues, ask your daughter's school counselor or pediatrician to refer you to a therapist or psychologist. There's no longer such a stigma about getting professional psychological help, and even if they see someone against their will at first, most girls are thankful to have an objective adult to talk to. "I think everyone should see a counselor if they're having an issue," says thirteen-year-old Alex, who saw a therapist after a friend attempted suicide. "No one except me knew that my friend had done that, so not only was it hard to deal with, but it was also a secret.

Just letting the counselor know how I feel—afterward, I just felt better about myself. Just to have someone tell me that I wasn't screwing up is pretty much all I needed to hear."

Hayley, a Washington seventh grader, sees a therapist regularly and says she's grateful for that support. "She has all of these exercises for calming yourself and focusing your mind, and teaches me not to focus on the bad things," she says. "She's helped me learn how to take care of my stress and worries. She might not always agree with me, but she's not afraid to tell me the truth. She'll suggest things, but doesn't tell me I have to do them."

Being able to talk openly and honestly about whatever they're going through, with a trained adult who can offer

Just-Been-There Advice:
I See a Therapist

"People make counseling into a bad thing, but it's not. I tell the middle school girls I work with whose parents want them to go that it doesn't mean you're crazy. I see mine twice a month; she's someone who can listen to your feelings and really help you understand why you're feeling them. A counselor can legitimize your feelings and say, 'You're feeling this because this happened.' She helped me realize that my feelings are what they are, and they're not going to change just because I want them to. I'm a lot more positive now than I was when I started."

—Audrey, sixteen

genuine help, is exactly what's needed when things get really tough.

I consider myself extremely lucky that I haven't been forced to deal with these kinds of major life issues. But I do think that I could've easily gone down some of these roads to depression. I saw a lot of my girlfriends battle these issues, and I've seen it with some of the girls I work with. Girls are much more prone to internalize pain than boys are, and this can often lead to unhealthy behavior.

What was the difference between my friends' situations and mine? We were all working with different life circumstances, but I really believe that the things that helped keep me stable and allowed me to continue making good choices were the three takeaways to downplay the drama. Through dance, working with Amanda, and having older mentors, I was able to stay healthy throughout middle school. If I hadn't had a slightly older mentor and a number of adult influences who served as stand-in parents, if I hadn't had such a strong after-school activity like dance, and if I hadn't been so committed to my work at the literacy center, I really don't know where I'd be today.

The three takeaways to downplay the drama can work on different levels. They're preventative measures that can help girls walk a steady path and keep them feeling whole throughout these years. But they're also a way to heal and to regroup from painful situations. I've seen lots of girls dealing with these issues bounce back much more quickly when they had a strong relationship with an older girl, an anchor activity, and were volunteering a helping hand. It's never too late to implement these three elements in a girl's life. One of my favorite middle schoolers was recently dealing with some big family problems, but I kept steering her toward the sport she loves to play, and now, both her mom and I see such a difference in her strength and resilience.

These takeaways won't save your middle schooler from encountering any of the issues we talk about here. But I guarantee that they will better help her deal with them and make her a stronger, more grounded person so that if she does hit any of these larger roadblocks, she'll be much more equipped to handle them.

Try This: Help Her Handle Family Drama or Depression

Divorce

- **Write a letter.** Encourage your middle school girl to write a letter to one or both of her parents describing her feelings about the situation. Don't read these letters (unless she asks you to); just give her the opportunity to express her emotions.
- **Stay connected.** Create a family Web site where you can upload pictures and blog about your days. This can be a great way for separated parents to stay connected to your tween.

General Family Drama

- **Hold family meetings.** Designate a time to talk out any family issues. End your meetings by asking each family member to say something kind about each of the others.

Depression

- **List the negative and the positive.** If your middle schooler seems to be dealing with depression, take her to a neutral location like a local coffee shop and ask her to write down the things in her life that contribute to these feelings. Talk with her about why she's listed each reason. On a new piece of paper, ask her to list all the positive aspects of her life.

The Bottom Line

- It can be extra hard for tweens to handle big family issues and serious problems, since they're already dealing with so much change. They're old enough to know if something's not right at home, but they don't have the independence (or the opportunities for escape) of high schoolers.

- Parents might think they're shielding their middle schoolers by avoiding the truth of what's happening or pretending that everything's okay. But tweens say that when their parents are honest and straightforward, they're able to trust them more.

- A therapist or counselor can offer girls an objective point of view and a safe space to honestly share their feelings.

- The three takeaways to downplay the drama are effective measures to help avoid many of the topics discussed throughout the book—but they're also healing mechanisms that will help girls survive their hardest times.

Afterword

Throughout *The Drama Years*, I've let tweens and teens speak for themselves, telling you how they think you can best help girls survive middle school. I hope their stories have touched you and that through them you can better understand, relate to, and feel compassion for the middle school girl in your life.

I also hope that you've come away with an understanding of why the three takeaways to downplay the drama—giving your girl an anchor activity, a helping hand, and an adopted older sister—are so essential for building strong, healthy middle schoolers. These three things changed my life and the lives of so many girls around me, and I know they can be transformative for your tween too.

The issues discussed in this book are pressing and very real—and as technology evolves at lightning speed, affecting how girls interact with one another, and as the many stresses on girls continue to mount up, it's imperative that everyone who works with tween girls try to help them: they need you *now*. And whatever you do, whether it's finding a Girl Talk chapter or just trying to support her journey to being a good friend, please remember this: you're doing more than helping one girl. You're investing in *all* girls. If we can start now to convince today's girls to let go of the drama, to truly try to be kind to one another, and to recognize (and stand up for) their inherent inner

253

worth, we'll eventually see a generation of kind, thoughtful women.

Your journey toward understanding your middle schooler doesn't have to end here. At www.thedramayears.org, you'll find a whole community of parents ready to share their thoughts, opinions, and anecdotes about these issues. Have you successfully implemented this advice with your middle schooler? Are you wondering what other parents are doing to help their girls? If you have a story to tell or questions to ask, visit the Web site and talk to us! There are also activities, resources, and forums for readers to discuss their own ideas, and so much more.

If *The Drama Years* has piqued your interest in involving your middle school or high school girl in Girl Talk, we'd love to have you! Please go to thedramayears.org to find a chapter near you or to learn how to start your own.

Sources

Chapter 2: I'm So Stressed!
Handling Everyday Anxiety

39 *In fact, a 2009 study from the American Psychological Association:* American Psychological Association, "Stress in America 2009" (Washington, D.C.: American Psychological Association, 2009), http://www.apa.org/news/press/releases/stress-exec-summary.pdf. "Nearly half (45 percent) of teens ages 13–17 said that they worried more this year, but only 28 percent of parents think their teen's stress increased, and while a quarter (26 percent) of tweens ages 8–12 said they worried more this year, only 17 percent of parents believed their tween's stress had increased" (p. 4).

41 *When* Seventeen *magazine conducted a major survey*: "Generation Perfect," Whitney Joiner, *Seventeen* magazine, October 2005.

42 *And in a survey of 3,000 middle school and high school students*: "In general, girls report far more school-related stress than do boys. They believe that to be successful, they have to be extraordinary in every area of their lives: academic, social, extracurricular, and appearance. . . . More than 2/3 of girls in middle school say they 'usually' or 'always' pressure themselves to succeed." http://www.ronicohensandler.com/teen_stress_survey.html.

Chapter 5: BFFs, Frenemies, and Mean Girls:
What It Means to Be a Friend

133 *A 2011 poll from MTV and Associated Press found that fifty percent of teens:* "More than half (56%) of those surveyed say they have experienced abuse through social and digital media," 2011 AP-MTV Digital Abuse Study, Executive Summary, p. 1.

Sources

Chapter 6: "It's Not Just Cooties Anymore":
Love and Relationships

161 *According to a 2008 study released by Liz Claiborne Inc. and LoveIs Respect.org:* Love Is Respect.org, National Domestic Violence Hotline, and Liz Claiborne, *Tween and Teen Dating Violence Abuse Study*, February 2008, http://www.loveisrespect.org/wp-content/uploads/2008/07/tru-tween-teen-study-feb-081.pdf. "Nearly half of all tweens (47%)—and more than one in three 11- to 12-year-olds (37%) [not charted]—say they have been in a boyfriend/girlfriend relationship." (p. 6).

Chapter 9: Getting Serious:
When the Drama Is Very Real

244 *Statistics about tween depression are hard to come by, but we know that about 14 percent of teenagers:* The NSDUH (National Survey on Drug Use and Health) Report, published by SAMHSA (Substance Abuse and Mental Health Services Administration), *Depression Among Adolescents*, December 2005http://oas.samhsa.gov/2k5/youthDepression/youthDepression.htm.

245 *The term* cutting *encompasses many different forms of self-injury:* Patricia A. Adler and Peter Adler, *The Tender Cut: Inside the Hidden World of Self-Injury* (New York: NYU Press, 2011), p. 1.

245 *No studies focus solely on girls between the ages of eleven and thirteen:* Charles Goodstein, clinical associate professor of psychiatry at New York University School of Medicine, "Cutting: The New-Age Anorexia?" *Discovery,* http://health.howstuffworks.com/mental-health/mental-disorders/cutting.htm.

245 *Nineteen-year-old actress and musician Demi Lovato: 20/20,* ABC, April 22, 2011. Excerpted in "Demi Lovato Interview: Teen Star Opens Up on Bulimia, Cutting Issues," April 19, 2011, http://abcnews.go.com/Entertainment/demi-lovato-interview-teen-star-opens-bulimia-cutting/story?id=13405090.

Resources

If you're interested in learning more about the topics covered in *The Drama Years*, check out these resources. You'll also find suggestions for where to find more information for issues we didn't cover:

Chapter One: Being True to Her:
Self-Esteem, Self-Awareness, and Self-Respect

Books

Chicken Soup for the Teenage Soul: Teens Talk Middle School, by Jack Canfield, Mark Victor Hansen, Madeline Clapps, and Valerie Howlett (Cos Cob, CT: Chicken Soup for the Soul, 2008).

The Curse of the Good Girl: Raising Authentic Girls with Courage and Confidence, by Rachel Simmons (New York: Penguin Press, 2009).

Girls Inc. Presents: You're Amazing! A No-Pressure Guide to Being Your Best Self, by Claire Mysko (Avon, MA: Adams Media, 2008).

The Good Girl Revolution: Young Rebels with Self Esteem and High Standards, by Wendy Shalit (New York: Ballantine, 2008).

My Feet Aren't Ugly: A Guide to Loving Yourself from the Inside Out, by Debra Beck (New York: Beaufort Books, 2007).

Real Girl/Real World: Tools for Finding Your True Self, by Heather M. Gray, Samantha Phillips and Ellen Forney (Berkeley, CA: Seal Press, 1998).

Respect: A Girl's Guide to Getting Respect and Dealing When Your Line Is Crossed, by Courtney Macavinta and Andrea Vander Pluym (Minneapolis, MN: Free Spirit Publishing, 2005).

Reviving Ophelia: Saving the Selves of Adolescent Girls, by Mary Pipher (New York: Riverhead Books, 1994).

Schoolgirls: Young Women, Self-Esteem and the Confidence Gap. Peggy Orenstein (New York: Doubleday/Anchor, 1994).

Resources

Sites and Organizations

Girl Talk: www.desiretoinspire.org
Girls Inc: www.girlsinc.org
Girls on the Run: www.girlsontherun.org
gURL.com: www.gurl.com
Respect RX: www.respectrx.com

Chapter Two: I'm So Stressed!
Handling Everyday Anxiety

Books

The Anxiety Workbook for Teens: Activities to Help You Deal with Anxi-ety and Worry, by Lisa M. Schab (Oakland, CA: New Harbinger Publications, 2008).

Dealing with the Stuff That Makes Life Tough: The 10 Things That Stress Girls Out and How to Cope with Them, by Jill Zimmerman Rut-ledge (New York: McGraw-Hill, 2003).

The Stress Reduction Workbook for Teens: Mindfulness Skills to Help You Deal with Stress (Instant Help), by Gina M. Biegel (Oakland, CA: New Harbinger Publications, 2010).

Stressed-Out Girls: Helping Them Thrive in the Age of Pressure, by Roni Cohen-Sandler (New York: Penguin, 2006).

The Triple Bind: Saving Our Teenage Girls from Today's Pressures, Ste-phen Hinshaw (New York: Ballantine, 2009).

Chapter Three: Who Has What:
Name Brands, Materialism, and Competition

Books

Born to Buy: The Commercialized Child and the New Consumer Culture, by Juliet Schor (New York: Scribner, 2005).

Packaging Girlhood: Rescuing Our Daughters from Marketers' Schemes, by Sharon Lamb and Lyn Mikel Brown (New York: St. Martin's Griffin, 2007).

Resources

Sites and Organizations

Do Something: www.dosomething.org
Volunteer Match: www.volunteermatch.org

Chapter Four: Her Body, Herself:
Body Image, Weight, and the Pressure to Be Pretty

Books

The Body Scoop for Girls: A Straight-Talk Guide to a Healthy, Beautiful You, by Jennifer Ashton (Avery, 2009).
Deal with It! A Whole New Approach to Your Body, Brain and Life as a gURL, Esther Drill, Rebecca Odes and Heather McDonald (Gallery Books, 1999).
Do I Look Fat in This? by Jessica Weiner (New York: Pocket Books, 2007).
Rock What You've Got: Secrets to Loving Your Inner and Outer Beauty, by Katherine Schwarzenegger (Voice, 2010).
You'd Be So Pretty If . . . : Teaching Our Daughters to Love Their Bodies— Even When We Don't Love Our Own, by Dara Chadwick (Burlington, VT: Da Capo, 2009).

Sites and Organizations

Center for Young Women's Health: www.youngwomenshealth.org
Dove's Campaign for Real Beauty: www.dove.us/Social-Mission/ campaign-for-real-beauty.aspx
Miss Representation documentary: misrepresentation.org
National Women's Health Information Center: www.womenshealth .gov/bodyimage/
Operation Beautiful: www.operationbeautiful.com

Resources

Books

How to Win Friends and Influence People for Teen Girls, by Donna Dale Carnegie (New York: Touchstone, 2005).

Mean Chicks, Cliques, and Dirty Tricks: A Real Girl's Guide to Getting through the Day with Smarts and Style, by Erika V. Shearin Karres (Avon, MA: Adams Media, 2004).

The Narcissism Epidemic: Living in the Age of Entitlement, Jean M. Twenge, Ph.D., and W. Keith Campbell, Ph.D. (New York: Free Press, 2009).

Odd Girl Out: The Hidden Culture of Aggression in Girls, by Rachel Simmons (Wilmington. MA: Mariner Books, 2003).

Queen Bees and Wannabees: Helping Your Daughter Survive Cliques, Gossip, Boyfriends and New Realities of Girl World, by Rosalind Wiseman (New York: Three Rivers Press, 2002).

Totally Wired: What Teens and Tweens Are Really Doing Online, by Anastasia Goldstein (New York: St. Martin's Griffin, 2007).

Sites and Organizations

A Thin Line: www.athinline.org/

Delete Digital Drama: abcfamily.go.com/movies/cyberbully/delete -digital-drama

Finding Kind documentary: findingkind.indieflix.com

It Gets Better: www.itgetsbetter.org

Kind Campaign: www.kindcampaign.com

The Megan Meier Foundation: www.meganmeierfoundation.org

Rachel's Challenge: www.rachelschallenge.org

Say It 2 My Face: www.sayit2myface.org

Stop Cyberbullying: www.stopcyberbullying.org

Resources

Chapter Six: "It's Not Just Cooties Anymore": Love and Relationships

Books

The Real Truth About Teens and Sex: From Hooking Up to Friends with Benefits—What Teens Are Thinking, Doing, and Talking About, and How to Help Them Make Smart Choices, Sabrina Weill (Perigee Trade, 2006).

A Smart Girl's Guide to Boys: Surviving Crushes, Staying True to Yourself and Other Stuff, by Nancy Holyoke (Middleton, WI: American Girl Publishing, 2001).

Talking about Boys: Real-Life Advice from Girls Like You, A Girl's World Productions and AGirlsWorld.com (New York: Three Rivers Press, 2001).

Chapter Seven: Dealing with *You:* Relating with Parents and Other Adults

Books

Five Conversations You Must Have with Your Daughter, by Vicki Courtney (Nashville, TN: B&H Books, 2008).

A Smart Girl's Guide to Understanding her Family: Feelings, Fighting and Figuring It Out (American Girl), by Amy Lynch (Middleton, WI: American Girl Publishing, 2009).

Chapter Eight: It's Not Fair! Boundaries and Consequences

Books

Get Out Of My Life, But First Could You Drive Me and Cheryl to the Mall? by Anthony E. Wolf (New York: Farrar, Straus and Giroux, 1991).

The Parent's Guide to Texting, Facebook and Social Media: Understanding the Benefits and Dangers of Parenting in a Digital World, by Shawn Edgington (Dallas, TX: Brown Books, 2011).

Resources

Books

The Divorce Workbook for Teens: Activities to Help You Move beyond the Break Up, by Lisa M. Schab (Oakland, CA: Instant Help, 2008).
A Smart Girl's Guide to Her Parents' Divorce: How to Land on Your Feet When Your World Turns Upside Down, by Nancy Holyoke and Scott Nash (Middleton, WI: American Girl Publishing, 2009).
The Tender Cut: Inside the Hidden World of Self-Injury, by Patricia A. Adler and Peter Adler (New York: NYU Press, 2011).

Sites and Organizations

S.A.F.E. (Self Abuse Finally Ends) Alternatives: www.selfinjury.com
To Write Love on Her Arms: www.twloha.com

Other Serious Topics

Dating Abuse/Sexual Abuse

Love Is Respect: www.loveisrespect.org
National Domestic Violence Helpline: www.ndvh.org
One Love Foundation: http://www.joinonelove.org/
Rape, Abuse and Incest National Network: www.rainn.org
The Safe Space: www.thesafespace.org

Drug and Alcohol Abuse

The Anti-Drug: www.theantidrug.com
Ask, Listen, Learn: www.asklistenlearn.com
The Century Council: www.centurycouncil.org
Check Yourself: www.checkyourself.com
The Cool Spot: www.thecoolspot.gov

Resources

Eating Disorders

Books

What's Eating You: A Workbook for Teens with Anorexia, Bulimia, and Other Eating Disorders, by Tammy Nelson (Oakland, CA: New Harbinger Publications, 2008).

Sites and Organizations

National Eating Disorders Association: www.nationaleatingdisorders .org
The Renfrew Center Foundation: www.renfrew.org
Something Fishy: www.something-fishy.org

Suicide

National Hopeline Network: www.hopeline.com
S.A.V.E: www.save.org
The Trevor Project: www.thetrevorproject.org

Tween/Teen Sexuality

National Campaign to Prevent Teen and Unplanned Pregnancy: www .nationalcampaign.org
Planned Parenthood. www.plannedparenthood.org
Sex, etc.: www.sexetc.org
StayTeen.org: www.stayteen.org

Acknowledgments

We couldn't have written *The Drama Years* without the help of some amazing people. First and foremost, thanks to our agent, Brettne Bloom, for introducing us (a perfect match!), helping us dream up this project, and believing in it from day one. Thanks to the fantastic team at Free Press: Dominick Anfuso, Wylie O'Sullivan, Jill Siegel, Carisa Brunetto, Claire Kelley, the design team, the sales and marketing team—and especially our wonderful editors, Alessandra Bastagli and Sydney Tanigawa, who helped clarify our vision.

Most of all, we thank the incredibly smart, thoughtful, fabulous girls whose voices make up this book. Thank you for your time, your generosity, and, above all, your honesty. Whatever wisdom adults gain from *The Drama Years* comes from you! Thanks as well to the great and supportive parents, teachers, and counselors who agreed to let us interview their girls and worked hard to fit our conversations into busy schedules.

Haley would also like to thank ...

It is with the utmost humility that I express my gratitude to all of you who have made this book a reality. You have all graciously circled around me and loved me through the best of days and the worst of days. You have shown me that with the right people in your life guiding you, life's greatest obstacles are merely stepping stones that guide you to your dreams. No one person could possibly do this alone, and I am honored to say thank you to each of you.

Acknowledgments

First and foremost, I would like to thank God for all the wonderful people he has placed in my life. I do not believe in coincidence and know that each of you (yes, even the mean girls) has been an important piece of this story. Your presence throughout this journey has been a true gift and I am so grateful to God for inspiring Girl Talk and *The Drama Years*.

Thank you to the five men (all dads themselves) who have made the past ten years possible. W. T. Henry, my high school headmaster, for saying yes to my Girl Talk dream as a tenth grader in 2002. Doug Brown, president of Brown Bag Marketing, for allowing your team to take a big pro bono leap of faith when I came to you as a nineteen-year-old with a big idea and no budget. You and your team brought Girl Talk to life and continue to give us wings. Ron Bell, Girl Talk's founding sponsor, for trusting me, as a college sophomore, with the most generous donation from your family foundation and for your continued support. Your wisdom has guided me down the right path, and I am forever grateful for you. I hope the return on your investment has made you proud. Bob Davis, managing director at PIVOT Strategic Marketing, for being my mentor and my friend and for showing me that even the biggest dreams do come true. I am forever grateful for your support, wisdom, and genuine belief in the mission of Girl Talk. Dominick Anfuso, vice president, editor in chief at Free Press/ Simon & Schuster, for truly understanding my vision and goal for this book—simply to help make middle school easier for girls.

To the women in my life who continue to pour into me and model the importance of having female mentors. You show me the positive impact one woman can make in the life of another woman, and you inspire me daily to model this to young girls who will soon be women like you. Thank you Mary Goodyear Adams, Lynne Dale, Christine Davis, Kara Friedman, Jennifer Grizzle, Julie Huff, Susan Hughes, Erin Levin, Erynn Mozier, Lori Oliver, Jen Pair, Laura Pitsikoulis, and Kelli Ritter.

To those of you who loved me through my drama years and

whose unconditional love and support is a significant part of the Girl Talk story. Each of you has had a profound impact on my life. Thank you Kiki Amanatidis, Drew Aultman, Ralph Blackman, Bell family, Valerie Benton, Teresa Breen, LeDonna Bowling, Brown family, Burt family, Lanier Clark, Gene Clerkin, Frances and Jannekia Collins, Cathy Coward, Davis family, Hamilton family, Head family, Ruth Henry, Huff family, Joy Hungate, Bobby Joiner, Carol and Parks Jones, Mark Kasperowicz, Keeney family, Michelle Kelley, Cindy and Bill "Papa" Kilpatrick, Leslie Kimball, Mary Catherine Kinney, Caleigh Lentz, Debbie Lentz, Susan Lentz, Dustin Lovingood, Carolyn Martin, Mathis family, Pam McDonald, Earlene Neeley, Darron O'Bonnon, Onley Family, Sarah Orgel, Sharon Presley, Christie Riles, Judi Sikora, Keli Smurda, Molly and Bill Swan, Chandra Czape Turner, Maryashley Whitaker, Lisa and Vernon Whitaker, Wicker family, and Wright family.

A sincere thank you to the Girl Talk girls, leaders, parents, and teachers who invested their time, wisdom, and guidance in *The Drama Years*. Your expert advice has been the key ingredient throughout this book.

A very special thank you to our Girl Talk team, board of directors, advisory board, teen advisory board, and volunteers for being my guardrails and my sanity, and most of all for being there for me personally and professionally throughout this project.

To my family, who offers endless support and encouragement. My parents, Tonya and Bert; my brother, Will; and my sister, Kelly—you each have a piece of my heart that beats just for you. I am so grateful for all that we have shared together and look forward to all that is to come. A special thank you to my mom, for being the first to listen to my Girl Talk idea (at our local IHOP in Albany, Georgia) ten years ago. You instantly believed in my vision, and by doing so, you helped ignite a dream that now lights up all over the world. To my extended Dozier family, Ed, Susan, Jon, Brenda, Miles, and Camille, thank you for your genuine love, support, and understanding. A big thank you to those of you who have truly become family—you know you who are. Thank you for enriching my life in all the ways that you do.

Whitney Joiner, my copilot, thank you for all that you have poured into this project. Your friendship is a gift, and I admire you more than you know. I appreciate your walking alongside me every step of the way.

Paul, my husband, I love you. Thank you for your unconditional love, late night listening, and patience when I just couldn't find a stopping point. Most of all, thank you for being my rock and for dreaming with me. Each day spent with you is a blessing.

To you, the reader, I hope you see the difference that a person with positive energy and support can have on another person's life. I hope you are that person in someone's life and that you also have many who encourage you in your life.

And Whitney would like to thank...

My mother, Brenda Overturf, whose feedback was invaluable and whose thirty-plus years in middle school education and literacy came in handy multiple times while reporting the book. For general excellency in the support department, huge thanks to Daniel Chamberlin. Thanks also to my brother, Andrew Joiner, and my grandparents, Nancy and Paul Scott. Other super supporters: Chris Hillen, Daeryl Holzer, Rachel and Chase Lindley, Monica Khemsurov, Tom Michael and the staff at Marfa Public Radio, Sahra Motalebi, David Nichtern, Ethan Nichtern, Liz Webler Rowell, Larry Smith, Matthew Steinfeld, and Carol Whipple. Haley, you've been an incredible partner every step of the way; I can't thank you enough. And most of all, thank you to the wonderful girls I worked with over the past few years. Over and over again, I was blown away by your honesty, your wisdom, and your insight. You're all amazing!

Index

Index

Boys. *See also* Romantic
  relationships
  desire to impress, 94,
    96–102
  reluctance to discuss with
    parents, 184–85
Bullying, 10, 73. *See also*
  Cyberbullying; Teasing

Campbell, Keith, 142
Celebrities, influence of, 66
Cell phones, 3, 215, 221. *See
  also* Texting
Chores, 212, 220
Cohen-Sandler, Roni, 42
Competition
  body image/appearance
    and, 101
  materialism and, 72, 74–77
Compromise, 227–28
Compromise list, 207–8
Computers, 221. *See also*
  Cyberbullying; Social
  networking sites
Confidence teams, 35
Conformity
  body image/appearance
    and, 93
  materialism and, 71, 75–76
  self-esteem and, 20
CosmoGIRL! magazine, 153
Creative pursuits, 58
Curfew, 219
Cutting, 245–48
Cyberbullying, 3, 121–23,
  133, 134

DeGeneres, Ellen, 141
Depression, 10, 236, 237–38
  prevalence of, 244–45

suggestions for coping
  with, 246, 252
Digital abuse, 133. *See also*
  Cyberbullying
Divorce, 233–34, 235, 237,
  238, 239, 247, 251
  children caught in the
    middle of, 240–41
  discussing honestly, 242, 243

Eating disorders, 110. *See also*
  Weight, preoccupation
  with
Empathy, 23
Endorphins, 50, 113
Exercise, 114
Extracurricular activities,
  53–54. *See also* Anchor
  activity

Facebook, 214, 223–27
Failing forward, 44, 45
Failure, fear of, 43–45
Family meetings, 251
Family trauma, 10, 233–44
  helping children through,
    240–44, 251
  honest expression of
    feelings about, 242–44
Fey, Tina, 123
Frenemies, 10, 125, 138, 144
Friends, 10, 121–56, 185
  authenticity and, 142, 144
  BFFs, 136–37, 148
  body image/appearance
    and, 94–96, 106–7
  bonding over self-criticism,
    106–7
  changing and breaking
    with, 123–31

Index

Index

Index

Index

About the Authors

Haley Kilpatrick is the founder and executive director of Girl Talk, a nonprofit organization that establishes positive weekly peer-to-peer mentoring programs between high school and middle school girls. Girl Talk helps girls build self-esteem, develop leadership skills, and recognize the value in community service. Since its inception in 2002, Girl Talk has reached more than 40,000 girls in forty-three states and six countries. Haley has been featured on NBC's *The Today Show,* the NBC *Nightly News,* ABC's *Everyday Health,* and the *Huffington Post.* She was named one of CNN's Young People Who Rock, *Glamour*'s 2010 20 Women Changing the World Now, *Self*'s 2010 Women Doing Good, and *People*'s All-Stars Among Us. Inspired by her own middle school experience, Haley's goal is twofold: for every middle school girl to have access to a Girl Talk chapter in her community and to put an end to the cycle of middle school girl drama while planting the seed for future generations of kind, compassionate women.

Whitney Joiner, a former features editor at *Seventeen,* writes about issues related to teen girls and women for a variety of publications. Her work has appeared in *ELLE, Glamour, Marie Claire, Marie Claire Australia,* the *New York Times, Redbook, Salon, Teen Vogue, TIME,* and *Whole Living.* A graduate of Smith College, she lives in Marfa, Texas.